The Changing Years

Martin Morrissey

THE O'BRIEN PRESS

DUBLIN

The
Changing Years

A COUNTRY BOY GRADUATES to long trousers and his first Grand Dance in the days when the electric light was regarded as a dangerous innovation and marriages were still made in Lisdoonvarna.

MARTIN MORRISSEY'S second book is a fascinating chronicle of changing times in rural Ireland of the 1940s.

MARTIN MORRISSEY
Raised on a farm in west Clare, between the towns of Miltown-Malbay and Kilrush. Emigrated to New York in the late 1950s and worked there as a travel agent until his return to Ireland in the early 1970s, where he worked in Cork with a multinational company as sales and development manager. He is now a freelance travel agent, living in Clare.

Contents

First published 1992 by The O'Brien Press Ltd., 20 Victoria Road, Dublin 6.
Copyright © Martin Morrissey

10 9 8 7 6 5 4 3 2 1

British Library Cataloguing in Publication Data

ISBN 0-86278-279-1

The O'Brien Press receives assistance from the Arts Council
An Chomhairle Ealaíon

Cover Illustration: Cathy Henderson
Cover Design: Michael O'Brien
Colour Separations: The City Office, Dublin
Printing: The Guernsey Press Co. Ltd., Channel Islands

CHAPTER ONE

The Years of Change

FOR ALMOST A CENTURY, from the post-famine years to the 1950s, the daily lifestyle of rural Ireland remained basically unchanged. Over that long period, the lot of the small-farm community in general improved; abject poverty gradually gave way to better conditions, but nevertheless, the people continued to live in a high degree of drudgery and want. By the 1940s, the war years, their ability to survive had become a finely-tuned, skilful art. Survival became a victory in itself, and any changes, improvements or innovations were viewed with suspicion and distrust. However, changes did take place, and to those of us growing up in the '40s, they became a never-ending source of delight and curiosity.

The first big change that came our way was the introduction of electric light. Up to then we had made do in west Clare with the oil lamp. Very often even the oil lamp had to be quenched while the local shopkeeper awaited a fresh supply of precious paraffin and at such times we had to rely on the home-made candle. Wreckage from torpedoed cargo ships was washed ashore almost every day on the nearby coast – timber, bales of rubber and cotton and, now and then, a bale of hard yellow tallow.

A local entrepreneur devised a method of melting the

unrefined tallow and, with the use of a waxed piece of twine and the barrel of a bicycle pump, producing make-shift candles. Because the tallow had had a long immersion in sea water, the candles spluttered continuously, but they were considered a better option than sitting in darkness with only the light of the fire. We envied the town people who had the privilege of electric light at their fingertips.

Towards the end of the '40s, news appeared in the local paper that our area was being considered as the location for a pilot scheme to bring electricity to every house in the parish; this was given the official title of the rural electrification scheme. Farmers who had long before abandoned hope of politicians or government departments doing anything sensible now smiled ruefully, shaking their heads in wonder at this latest daft government plan. The general consensus of opinion at local level was that it was impractical and would not work and was, in short, a sheer waste of time and money!

A great many harboured doubts about their ability to meet the cost of this new luxury. They suspected that the offer of cheap electricity was only a sales gimmick to encourage them to join the scheme, after which the cost would soar. The withdrawal of the service at a later date because of their inability to pay large bills would not alone wound their pride but would also damage the good name of the family. Rather than openly admit their misgivings, they attacked the new scheme as being totally unnecessary and a downright danger to man and beast.

The subject provided a whole new topic of conversation at night-time. Some declared that electricity was 'not natural and went against all the known laws of God and man'. How such awesome power could run along a simple piece of wire was incomprehensible! People who had visited large towns recalled seeing the network of power lines along the side of the streets, and had noticed a very strange phenomenon. They knew that to touch a live power line meant instant death, yet birds could perch on the swaying wires without coming to any harm. This was conclusive proof that electricity could be unpredictable; it appeared to be selective in what it killed, or else God himself must have given birds a special immunity! Others were genuinely afraid that the wires would set fire to their thatched roofs. They feared that fallen wires during stormy weather would kill some of their cattle and, in those pre-insurance days, any loss was a total loss. But of all those fears, both genuine and imagined, the question of being able to afford the new service was the greatest.

The decades up to and including the 1940s were years of frugal self-sufficiency. Through hard work, careful management and with the support and co-operation of the neighbours, each farmer provided for his family. Most of the food on the table was home-grown. A pig, or two in the case of a large family, was fattened, killed and salted each year. The occasional goose or hen, with the rare luxury of fresh butcher's meat after a successful fair day, broke the monopoly enjoyed by salty bacon. With the deft use of needle and thread, articles of clothing were shortened, lengthened, let down or let out, darned, or even turned inside-out when faded. Outgrown trousers, shirts and jackets were refurbished and passed on as hand-me-downs to younger members of the family. A suit of clothes made of a serviceable navy-blue serge could last for twenty years, maybe even a lifetime.

Money, what little of it was available, was spent sparingly and sensibly. Apart from the necessary spending on food or clothing, there were other demands on the available cash, the demands of church and state. The moral obligation of contributing to church collections, on average about five shillings per collection, was a matter of integrity and pride. The legal obligation of paying rates to the local County Council had more serious undertones. The fear of a visit from the county sheriff for failure to pay the rates, and the ultimate fear of eviction, was a constant shadow over every small farmer. The rates, estimated each year, and based on the rateable valuation of each holding, were paid in two moieties or halves.

In our area on the west coast, the two biggest fair days of the year occurred on 9 March and 15 October. Long before daybreak, the local town would be packed with farmers from several miles around, each hoping to sell his few calves or yearlings. It was no accident and was indicative of the times that both of these very big fairs coincided with the gale days, the days on which the first and second moiety of the rates fell due. As each farmer sold his few cattle and received the money for them, he made his way to a house at the end of the main street where Paddy the rate collector had set up a temporary office for the day. He paid what was due and, clutching his precious receipt, usually made his way to a public house to join his neighbours in a celebratory bottle or two of stout. He was safe for another six months!

By the 1940s, while the fear of a visit from the sheriff

still existed, one other dark aspect of rural life, the role of the 'land grabber', had virtually disappeared. This was a fairly common feature of the nineteenth century landlord era when the holding of an evicted tenant farmer was taken over, or grabbed, by an unscrupulous fellow-tenant who had no misgivings about expanding his own holding to the misfortune of his neighbour.

Even more hated and feared than the landlord or the sheriff, the grabber was ostracised from the local community and the stigma was carried by his descendants for several generations. When the landlords faded into history and local authorities were established, a new generation of grabbers thrived on the misfortunes of others. Through a loop-hole in the law, an unscrupulous person could receive title to a holding, or more often part of a holding, by paying the sheriff any arrears in rates owed by a neighbour who had fallen on hard times.

While matters had improved slightly in the first few post-war years, it was against this background of some financial instability and worry that the local people had to consider joining the new electrification scheme. Even though no initial deposit was required, the fear of future sharp increases was uppermost in many of their minds. In a close-knit community where a person's private business was rarely private, they dreaded the ignominy of being disconnected.

A big promotion campaign was undertaken by the scheme and a large group of experienced sales people arrived from different parts of Ireland. Never had the area witnessed such an influx of strange accents as reasoned voices, from as far away as Cork, Mayo, Donegal or

Dublin, explained the benefits of electricity and tried to allay doubts and fears. Every house in the area was canvassed by two of the group and they were always accompanied by some respected local advocate in order to give credence to their case. The protracted canvass paid dividends as most of the householders decided to join the scheme.

The whole area then became a hive of industry as the scheme swung into operation. Gangs of men arrived from various parts of the country to work on the erection of poles and the hanging of cables. The strangers were warmly accepted by the locals and by the end of their first year many unfamiliar names appeared in the local marriage registers. Romance blossomed amid the forest of electricity poles that dotted the roadsides and crisscrossed the fields and meadows.

One immediate benefit from the scheme was the temporary employment given to a large number of local people, especially farmers' sons. For them it was a welcome relief to escape from the day-to-day drudgery of trying to make ends meet on a small farm. It was their first introduction to the strange worlds of commerce and industry. Never before did they have such a short working week, from eight in the morning until six in the evening and a half day on Saturdays! Never before had they received a weekly pay envelope! Some of them never returned to farming and this marked the first wave of the flight from the land, the migration from creamery cheque to pay cheque!

Watching the steady erection of the dark cresol-covered poles became a popular spectator sport. Progress was noted and discussed each night around the fire. New words crept into the vernacular. A closely contested game of cards was no longer just exciting, it was now 'electric', while a person might be described as being a 'real live-wire' or a 'bright spark'. For several months we followed the progress of the scheme from doorways, through kitchen windows or from the roadside, and it slowly became part of the environment. It was out there in the fields and on the roads each day, causing no disturbance to any of us. But this was only the lull before the storm. The next phase, preparing the houses and connecting them to the nearest pole, was about to begin.

The wiring of individual houses rekindled all the old doubts and controversies. Two electricians from the nearby town were appointed as official installers but, sensing a rich commercial harvest, a few others whose knowledge of electricity ranged from skimpy to non-existent, quickly jumped on the bandwagon. The standard rate was thirty shillings for each light fixture or power-point. This was quite expensive, especially when one recalls that the average price of a yearling calf at the time was about five pounds. Another sobering thought was that it was logical to assume that the more lights installed, the bigger the dreaded two-monthly bill. Both these factors ensured that very serious consideration was given to the question of the number of lights in each house.

On average, most households opted for a minimum number of lights until such time as they had a better picture of the expense involved. The kitchen was given top priority, being the central place in every home. Next came the rarely used parlour which was more of a concession to grandeur than to real necessity. A large number of people had the initiative and courage to install a light in every room, though others stopped short of that extravagance. Some parents put a light in their own bedroom but not in the others. They considered that their offspring would be tempted to waste too much electricity, especially as there was a commonly-held belief that the mere act of using the switch added a penny each time to the bill. In a house with several bedrooms, a light fitting was often put in the hallway, allowing light into several rooms through open doors or through the glass fanlight over the doors, a common feature in many old houses.

From inside the front door where the meter would be located, wires were strung along rafters to the various light points. The official installers did a professional job, using timber casing or ducting to conceal the wires. However, many of the would-be installers took short-cuts, simply clipping the wires onto the ceilings of parlours and bedrooms, leaving an unsightly and dangerous network of dark grey wires behind them. In a few houses, one such person simply attached some light fixtures to the ceilings without any connection whatsoever to the meter, demanded full payment and left! Many of the unfortunate householders accepted such shoddy workmanship as being the norm.

Usually only one power-point was installed, an outsize brown bakelite outlet suitable for an electric kettle or an electric iron, and was located high up on the wall, well out of the reach of curious children or of splashes of water. The electric kettle proved very popular but the iron was viewed as having a voracious appetite for electricity. One neighbour commented that 'when Mary plugs in the electric iron, that little hoor of a wheel in the meter goes round and round faster than a dog having a fit.'

Eventually the great day arrived, the day of the official switch-on. Thatched roofs were anxiously watched for any wisp of smoke as the much-feared power surged through the cables to each house. Without exception, every housewife rejoiced in the arrival of electricity. Eliminated would be the tedium of the daily polishing of the oil-lamp globe, the filling of the lamps with paraffin oil and the constant trimming of wicks. And despite one or two rumours that 'electric light is very bad for the eyes', they looked forward to the bright light with which they could comfortably sew or read.

On that first night, the light switch in the kitchen was ceremoniously turned on and we all peered at each other in the unaccustomed glare of the forty watt bulb suspended from the ceiling. It was wonderful. One could do one's homework in any part of the kitchen instead of being forced to move close to the oil-lamp on the wall near the fire. We basked in the miracle of modern technology. There was a festive spirit in the air. Our world was bright and would never again be dark.

Yes, our world was bright but in many cases it proved to be too bright! After the initial euphoria wore off, in almost every kitchen the eyes of house-proud mothers turned heavenwards, shocked and mortified. The new 'Ardnacrusha light' – the name associated with the hydroelectric scheme on the Shannon – cast its harsh brightness into every nook and cranny of the kitchen. Its illumination fell not only on the familiar kitchen features, but also on every cobweb lurking away in the dim corners. And there were many!

Most of the houses had been built in the second half of the nineteenth century and had thatched roofs. The thick stone-and-mortar walls supported a framework of rafters and laths that rose at a steep angle up to the peak of the roof. Here they were locked in place by a tie-beam that ran the full length of the roof. Long strips of sods or scraws, perhaps six inches or more in thickness, lay lengthwise on the framework of rafters and laths, insulating the roof against wind, rain and frost. A thick layer of thatch, preferably wheat straw, was pinned securely to the sods with the liberal use of scollops – U-shaped, sharpened rods of salley or bog-deal. After decades of thatching, many of those roofs were more than two feet thick.

In the kitchen, the overhead meat beam, with its suspended flitches of bacon, stretched from wall to wall. Above that, the pyramid of rafters and heat-blackened sods joined together in the upper recesses where the dim light of the oil-lamps never penetrated. Up there, amid the smoke-blackened timbers and sods, safely beyond the reach of duster or sweeping brush, generation after generation of spiders and small insects had carried on their daily business in peace and harmony. Thick veils of cobwebs had accumulated over the years, even further obscuring the mellow light of the lamps. But rural electrification was about to destroy the whole fabric of their secure and private world.

Down below, the housewives looked upwards in horror and shock as the Achilles' heel of their housekeeping, the city of cobwebs, was revealed for all to see. The following day, the big kitchen table was used as a platform from which a devastating attack was launched with long-handled brooms to sweep aside the thick veil of dust-laden cobwebs. From the spiders' point of view, it was a massacre! The flagged floor of the kitchen far below was littered with victims and streamers of tangled cobwebs.

Very shortly after the battle of the cobwebs, the housewife began to give subtle hints to less-than-interested husbands that the kitchen should be plastered. She often suggested that a low ceiling would save a lot of turf being burnt and would make the kitchen very warm and cosy. In due course, kitchen ceilings were covered over with sheets of plywood, though more affluent houses used the much more expensive, long, slender ceiling-boards. Unfortunately the now obtrusive meat beam had to be removed, joining the growing list of out-dated rural artifacts. The new ceiling was either painted or papered and became a symbol of the progressive, comfortable farmer.

After a few years, smoke and ashes from the open fire dulled the brightness of the new ceiling and the next step was inevitable. Up to this point, only the priests, teachers, shopkeepers and a few big farmers had had a range in their kitchens, big black ones that had to be constantly polished with range polish or blackening. A new, cream No. 8 range became the dream of every housewife! To their husbands they pressed their case, not in terms of grandeur but on economic grounds, pointing out that the small firebox would only take three or four sods of turf to fill. So the new ranges were installed. They were a boon to the housewife and removed a great deal of the hard work involved in baking, cooking and fire management.

The compact range, replacing the wide open hearth, left plenty of space on either side for two timber presses which were ideal for airing clothes. However, the visiting neighbours who came on *cuaird* each night felt that sitting around a range with the blaze hidden from view was not quite the same as the open hearth, and that much of the mystique was lost forever.

Gradually, further improvements and innovations were introduced. The flagged kitchen floors were levelled and covered with linoleum, silencing the ring of the dancers' feet in the set-dance. By the mid-'60s, back-kitchens or sculleries were being added. Electric cookers were installed there as the traditional work of the housewife moved from the kitchen to the scullery. The old kitchen was no longer a working kitchen; in fact it had gradually become a livingroom. As farmers' fortunes soared in the '70s, many of the old farmhouses were replaced by the new trend in modern house styles, the often characterless, but efficient, bungalow.

No longer could a neighbour lift the latch and walk in for a chat or a friendly cup of tea. Now an illuminated electric door-chime greeted them at the safety-locked door. Close co-operation and interaction between neighbours, the most striking features of the small-farm culture, were being slowly eroded. The hard-earned affluence of improved farming conditions was steadily replacing community dependence with individual independence, and the imported values of privacy and independence

were gradually breaking up the huge landmass of neigh-
bourliness into archipelagoes of self-sufficient islands.

CHAPTER TWO

My First Holiday

ONE OF MY FATHER'S older sisters, Liz, was married in his native parish of Cooraclare about six miles away from where we lived. In contrast to our own family where I was an only child, Liz had seven daughters. Mai, Della and Anna had embarked on nursing careers in Waterford, Lily was a legal secretary in Kilrush, Margaret worked at home, Eileen joined the post office after finishing secondary school and Teresa, who was about my own age, was still in school. They visited us regularly and in time, I came to regard them almost as sisters. They were a happy family and loved a good laugh. I can safely say without fear of contradiction that in all our years of close friendship, we never had even a minor argument!

My father was especially close to his sister Liz. She had played a major part in raising him, their father having died of pneumonia shortly after Dad was born. She was a very gentle soft-spoken lady with a great sense of humour. I can still picture her sitting by the fire with her arms folded over her cross-over apron, shaking with laughter as she related some story or other about my Dad when he was a boy. As a young boy, I found it very difficult to visualise my father as anything other than an adult, but Aunt Liz introduced me to a side of him of which I was totally unaware. It wasn't easy to accept that my strict Dad was once a small boy, 'full of devilment' as she termed it!

I had received invitations on several occasions to spend part of my school holidays in my aunt's house, but all entreaties fell on deaf ears at home. I accepted it as a lost cause! I guess I was about ten years old when Mother and Dad finally relented, following strong representations on my behalf by my cousins Della and Eileen. Dad promised them that he would take me with him when he made his Christmas visit to see Liz, her husband Paddy and all the girls. I was told that I could stay with them for two nights. This, I discovered much later, was a ruse to dispel any possible attacks of homesickness!

As the big day approached I hardly slept for excitement. I bragged to my school friends that I was going all the way to Cooraclare for my first holiday. The very thought of it gave me a sensation of foreign travel and adventure. My good friends next door, Eileen and her brother Michael, were informed about the great event. But at school I was forced to take a lot of teasing about staying in a house with seven girls. It was a sobering thought and suddenly my excitement became tinged with pangs of apprehension. I had always been accustomed to playing on my own except when at school. I had my own small bedroom, off the kitchen, and had the free run of the house and yard, inventing my own games and being able to switch from one game to another without first seeking the approval of other playmates. Of course, being an only child had its disadvantages too. Should a window be 'accidentally' broken with a stone or a ball, there was only one suspect – and you were it! And, of course, there was no opportunity to share, or if possible, avoid, the countless little chores that had to be done around a farmhouse, bringing in turf for the night fire, going for the cows or calves, carrying water from the well or picking potatoes in the autumn.

I had found that one of the biggest disadvantages of being an only child involved a simple game of football in the field at the back of the house. Kicking the ball as far as I could gave me a great feeling, but having to chase it each time all the way across the field took much of the fun from the game. It was also exhausting! I soon discovered that it was much less demanding to kick for height rather than distance.

But being on my own in that little field had a much more positive side. Given the right circumstances, a child's imagination knows no boundaries. I played the part of all my heroes in that small field. Depending on the whim of the moment, I 'became' goalkeeper Danno O'Keeffe of Kerry, Joe Keohane, Jimmy Smyth, Christy Ring or Jim Brosnan! My non-stop imitation of Michael O'Hehir ensured that my hero of the moment was playing an 'absolute blinder'. High balls were 'plucked from the clouds', amazing solo-runs split defences wide open, sidesteps were brilliantly executed, leaving opponents standing in open-mouthed admiration, great goals or points were scored while Danno O'Keeffe or Seán Wynne from Mayo made some spectacular diving saves in crowded goalmouths. What excitement! There were times when it was even too much for Michael O'Hehir himself!

So here I was, from the great independence of my life, going on holidays to a crowded house.

And with seven girls in one house, things were going to be very crowded indeed. To make matters worse, some of them were grown-ups like Eileen next door! These were all big worries which, of course, I had to conceal. Any display of anxiety might result in the withdrawal of the long-sought permission. Me and my big mouth. I had to go through with it now because I had told too many people. Maybe, just maybe, it would turn out all right.

On St Stephen's Day when all my school friends were going around the neighbourhood dressed as wrenboys, collecting pennies for sweets and lemonade, Dad tackled the big mare, Grey Fann, to the trap. His visit to his sister would be rather brief as he had to return in time for the evening chores. Mother had packed my bag with several changes of clothes. I pretended to be cheerful but inwardly I was feeling very lonely and was reluctant to leave the familiar surroundings. I said my goodbyes to Mother, to Fred the sheepdog and even to Teddy the small dog, who showed his usual disdain by turning his head the other way!

As Grey Fann trotted along the road, I kept up a constant chatter to hide my secret fears. After about five miles, we were already within Dad's former parish. He pointed out the long grey school which he had attended as a boy. As we went over the Cree bridge, he stopped Grey Fann for a moment to show me in the distance the long line of stepping stones that he had used every day to get across the river. When I questioned him, he explained that it was only a mile to school by using the fields and the river, whereas by road it was over two miles. He pointed out his old home, surrounded by trees, where his brother still lived, and in the far distance to the left, the Black Hill near which another sister lived. He would visit them in the new year. Memories flooded back to him as he identified the houses and recalled an anecdote about each one.

Before reaching the village of Cooraclare, we made a detour to the left for half-a-mile to visit the local cemetery. There, surrounded by a high stone wall, was the ruin of the old pre-famine church of Kilmacduane. I was scared to enter because of so many tombstones, but with Dad beside me I felt a little safer. Within the ruined church, where the high altar once stood, were the graves of his mother and father.

'It's nice to drop by and say a prayer for them and to wish them a happy Christmas,' he told me. Grandmother had died the previous year and it was hard to believe that she lay beneath that large flagstone! I could still see her soft round face with its quick smile, her wavy white hair, her cheerful voice telling me stories in her native Irish tongue, and her small slight figure, a little bent from the struggle of raising six children on her own on a small farm. I was no longer scared. I had a friend in that peaceful place.

A mile further on, we turned off the main road. From the crest of the first small hill, we could see my aunt's house about a half-mile away. Strung along that short stretch of winding road were seven or eight farmhouses. It was like an elongated small village. As we passed, old friends emerged from each house to greet Dad. He was among his own. I had always regarded the people of my own area as being most friendly and good-humoured but, on that first visit, I felt that the people of Cooraclare surpassed all my expectations. My opinion has not changed since!

We arrived at my aunt's house with its slated, hipped roof and a welcoming column of smoke ascending to the blue December sky. A shelter-belt of evergreens protected the western side of the newly-whitewashed house, giving it a picture-postcard effect. All the girls were home for Christmas and gave us a great welcome. It was like the return of the prodigal son, with a feast of a lunch waiting for us on the big kitchen table. It was a totally new experience for me to be in the middle of such a babble of voices. It reminded me a little of our own classroom when the master left the room for a few minutes. Aunt Liz, Paddy and Dad were in deep conversation by the fire while the seven girls and myself were huddled around the kitchen table in the middle of the room, telling jokes and having a great laugh. 'If this is what it's like having seven sisters, then I'm all in favour!' I thought to myself.

After about two hours, my father stood up, ready to begin the journey home. An icy hand of fear suddenly wrapped itself around me. What if Aunt Liz and my cousins did not want me in the house once Dad had disappeared around the bend of the road? Maybe they would throw me out the door? Would I be able to find my way home? Was this holiday idea a very big mistake? Would I ever see Mother and Dad again? Or Grey Fann? As Dad moved out of the farmyard, I ran after him, begging him not to forget me and to come back for me in two days. He calmed my fears and gave me his promise that he would be back. In our house, a promise was sacred.

My panic ebbed away. Aunt Liz put her arms around me and dried my tears, as Dad and Grey Fann disappeared down the avenue. I felt ashamed of my tears but the girls tactfully ignored my moment of weakness. They began to tell me about all the activities they had planned for my short holiday. It sounded quite interesting, I thought, and anyway two days would not be long passing!

Anna and Della took me for a walk around the farm-yard and fields. It was just like home with all the farm animals. They had pet names for their cows too. I told them the names of our cows. We were establishing some common ground! I told them about my school, about the master and the missus, while they told me about nursing and what it was like to be working in a big hospital. I had never been to a big hospital but having heard some of the work they had to do, I more or less decided there and then that I was not interested in being a doctor when I grew up.

Later on, Aunt Liz, Paddy and Margaret went to the sheds to milk the cows and do the evening chores. Aunt Liz maintained an age-old custom of abstaining from meat on St Stephen's Day as an act of penance for the holy souls. While the milking was in progress, Eileen and Teresa, with my wholehearted co-operation, raided the pantry where the cold remains of the Christmas dinner provided an irresistible temptation. Eileen estimated that three extra Hail Marys in our night prayers for the holy souls should restore the balance. Aunt Liz knew when she came in that there was something in the wind and we had great fun as she pretended to pressurise me into telling her what tricks the girls had been up to!

That night, with the mellow light of the oil-lamps shining on the Christmas decorations, several neighbours called in for a chat. My cousins loved dancing, and in a short time the kitchen table was pushed close by the wall and the big mahogany gramophone with its hinged lid was carried out from the parlour. The older girls had gone to the annual St Stephen's Night Grand Dance in the village of Kilmihil, five miles away, but the influx of neighbours more than made up for the shortfall. Very soon an impromptu house-dance was under way with four couples taking the floor for the first Caledonian, or Clare Set, of the evening. Even Aunt Liz joined in the festive spirit by supplying the music for several of the sets on her concertina. She was a happy person, surrounded by her family and friends. I soon discovered that it was the local custom to have 'a few sets' in each of the neighbours' houses each night of the Christmas holidays. That small rural settlement of seven or eight houses had a unique community spirit. Even though no blood-relationships existed between the families, they were like an extended family, very co-operative and devoid of any rancour or bickering.

I watched the girls dancing the sets and envied their skills because, although I loved the music, I had never tried dancing. Only too well aware of my own shortcomings, I resisted every effort to be dragged up on to the floor. Eileen promised me that, starting the following day, she was going to teach me how to dance the set. Despite my misgivings, I told her I would try. About midnight, the gramophone was put away and the neighbours walked in the frost-filled air to their homes, their path brightly lit by the soft moonlight.

Back in the kitchen, everybody knelt down and using a tilted-back chair as an armrest joined in the recitation of the rosary. Aunt Liz led the prayers and Paddy, with more hope than conviction, suggested that she 'go easy on the trimmings for one night' as it was so late. Being a guest, I was invited to recite the second decade. It proved to be almost more than I could handle. It took a supreme effort to be serious because I had Eileen and Anna at either side of me, each trying to make me laugh by pulling funny faces and giving me impish grins. I wavered on several occasions, but a convenient bout of coughing cloaked my acute desire to giggle at their antics. It was a relief when it was over. I don't think we fooled Aunt Liz.

As we stood up at the end to straighten our aching knees, she said to Eileen and Anna, 'Ye are two right raps, the pair of ye!' But there was a twinkle in her eye. Lying in bed, I reflected on the events of the afternoon and night and on how much I had enjoyed myself. As I drifted to sleep, I was wondering if Mother and Dad missed me and if they were lonely.

The following day was no less enjoyable. I was still being spoilt by the girls and I loved every minute of it. Unfortunately, Eileen had not forgotten her promise of the previous night – my dancing lessons began. It had looked very simple from the sidelines but now it seemed quite complex.

I understood her instructions perfectly but getting the message to my feet proved to be a major problem. Each foot weighed a ton and developed a mind of its own. I was quite willing to give up the ghost but Eileen persisted.

Several of the girls took it in turns to try to steer me around the floor with some semblance of gracefulness. And there was so much to remember – when to turn to your partner, when to slide and when to wheel in a full circle around the floor. After an hour, everybody was exhausted, but I was warned that the lessons would continue on the following day. I was amazed at their patience and perseverance in the face of such fumble-footed adversity. However, I found that my self-confidence had improved even if my dancing had not. That night we all went to Tadg's, a neighbour's house, where we were given a warm welcome with singing and dancing until midnight. I was loving every minute of this holiday.

I got up the next morning feeling a little sad. Just when I was getting to know all my cousins it was time to go home again. I missed Mother and Dad very much but the new companionship was great. Paddy returned from the creamery and came into the kitchen for a cup of tea. My glum face told its own story.

'Why are you so lonesome looking?' he asked me. 'Wait until I tell you my good news. While I was at the creamery, a man who was on his way to Kilrush brought a message from your Dad, that you could stay here for a couple of extra days. That is, of course, if you want to stay. Maybe you want to go home today?'

I quickly assured him that I wanted to stay on for the extra few days. 'I'll bring you home myself in a few days,' he told me. 'Anyway, I'll be going to wish your mother and dad a happy New Year.'

I was elated! The 'extra few days' became a week. But all good things must come to an end. A few days after

New Year's Day, I knew it was time to go home. It had been an unforgettable holiday, but the new school term was beckoning and the girls would soon be scattering. Paddy took me home in the pony and trap after a tearful farewell to the family at the gable of the house.

It was a strange feeling being home again, even though I had so many stories to tell Mother and Dad. The house seemed so quiet after the laughter, the noise and the fun of my holiday. It took a few days to adjust. I found it very difficult to return to playing games on my own. But school, despite all its obvious drawbacks, came to my rescue and by the end of the second day back in class, life returned to normal.

That first holiday laid the foundations for close friendships with my seven cousins, friendships that have endured the passage of time. For many years afterwards, I made the annual pilgrimage for a week to their home in Cooraclare. It was always the highlight of my year. They taught me many things, broadening my interests and my understanding of life. The only blot on their achievements was their failure to make me become a great set-dancer – despite their annual efforts, my two feet continued to glide ungracefully in the wrong direction at the wrong time!

By the time secondary schooling was over, we had all chosen to travel along different paths of life. One by one the girls married and began to raise their own families. Five of the girls have their homes and families in Tramore, and Margaret and Eileen remained in the Cooraclare area where I am still a fairly regular visitor. While we may have scattered all over the world, there has always existed among us a sense of belonging, a sense of family. I still believe that I came out best in the exchange. I gained seven 'sisters', while my cousins gained only one 'brother'!

CHAPTER 3

A Good Fire is
Half the Feeding!

IT WAS WELL INTO the second half of this century before there was any marked improvement in the daily life of the average small farmer. People were quite happy to survive from year to year and even the better-off small farmers lived only a fraction above subsistence level. Their main ambitions were to feed and clothe their family, have enough fodder for their livestock, be able to pay the rates and church dues, and have plenty of turf for the fire. The twin keys to survival were a rick of well-saved hay and a rick of good dry turf. Many would argue that saving the turf was even more important than the hay but they were, at least, of equal standing.

The expression 'a good fire is half the feeding' was often heard in those days. The big open fire was the hub of each farm. Not alone did it keep the house and its occupants warm and snug, it was also where all farm-cooking was done – potatoes for the hens, porridge of crushed maize, Injun' meal for the calves, and chopped root-crops for the fattening pig.

The production of a plentiful supply of turf was a long process, stretching from early spring to mid-summer or even later. In all, there were about six different stages —

stripping, cutting, turning, footing, putting out and bringing home. During a wet summer, the turning and footing might have to be repeated several times, giving extra hard work to the unfortunate farmer. To those of us who were still attending school, going to the bog seemed like the promise of high adventure. The freedom of the mountainside, the smell of the heather, the sounds of birds singing in the clear blue sky and, of course, the opportunity of missing a day from school, all gave one a great sense of well being. However, all those delights disguised the fact that a day in the bog could be a back-breaking experience that would make a person wish he was back in school with the master.

Up until the early 1940s, the farmers in our area bought the cutting of a supply of turf each year from people who owned large tracts of bogland, or mountain, on the other side of the parish. The negotiated price might be a cash settlement, an agreed number of workdays to the owner, or a certain number of horse-creels of dry turf for the owner's house. In practice, most deals involved a combination of two of these methods. Then, around 1940, the Land Commission divided a large section of mountainous bogland into small one-acre plots, assigning one to each farmer for a nominal annual rent. My father received one such plot in Mountrivers, six miles from home.

The Commission marked the boundaries of each plot and began building a network of primitive roads to provide access. Thick carpets of bushes were laid on the heather in long, narrow lines and were buried under a deep covering of earth, stones and gravel. Each year, new layers of shale gravel were added, strengthening the road surface, until horses and carts could travel safely on them.

It was a beautiful morning in mid-spring, but unfortunately I had to go to school. Dad was getting ready to cycle to the bog to begin the first stage of the turf-cutting. Before leaving, he sharpened the long vicious-looking hayknife with a three-cornered file until it was razor sharp. Covering the blade with some sacking, he tied it to the carrier at the back of the bicycle. A spade and pitchfork were tied securely with strong cord to the crossbar. Mother had prepared sandwiches and a bottle of tea, all neatly packed in the straw shopping-bag which he slung over the handlebars. Blessing himself at the small holy-water font by the front door, he took his leave with his much-used expression, 'We may as well make a start, *in ainm Dé.*'

Compared to other stages of the work, the stripping was relatively easy. Standing on top of the bank and about three or four feet from the edge of the little cliff formed by the previous year's cutting, Dad pumped the hayknife up and down, cutting through the thick layer of heather, withered grasses, compost and earth to a depth of more than a foot. Moving sideways with the blade, he cut, or raced, along the whole length of the bank. Retracing his steps, he then cut, towards the edge, a series of narrow strips. All this criss-cross cutting made the next step much easier. Using the spade and the pitchfork, each section was dug out and thrown into the bog-hole at the base of the little cliff. This served a dual purpose. In the short term the discarded debris helped to dry the bank by absorbing the excess pools of water in the boghole, and in the long term it accelerated the restoration of the bog to grassland by covering the wet peat soil with a thick layer of loam and fibrous materials. Dad now had the stripping completed and was ready for the next stage – the turf-cutting.

Three neighbours had volunteered their services to help Dad cut the turf. This was the normal system of neighbourly co-operation; in return, Dad would help each of them with their turf. As the operation was planned for the following Saturday, I asked, with only a faint hope of success, if I could go with them. I was delighted with his reply. 'You might be a big help to us,' he told me.

Mother baked several cakes, two on the griddle and one large one in the round iron oven or bastible. This large cake was her special occasion bread, prepared for the times when neighbours would gather to help Dad with tasks such as turf-cutting. She had her own recipe which included yeast and caraway seeds. A good-sized chunk of the remaining smoked ham was taken from its hook at the side of the chimney and roasted. When it had cooled, Dad cut it into thin slices while I hovered close by to rescue any broken slices. A big wicker basket was filled with bread, butter, ham, cutlery, enamel mugs, a big black kettle, a teapot, sugar and several bottles of milk. Mother was satisfied that there was more than enough in the basket for two tea-breaks and the main midday meal. On the Friday evening Dad had climbed up to the garret where he kept what Mother called, 'all his old trumpery' and returned with two turf-cutting winged spades, or *slauns*, which he cleaned and sharpened with great care.

All the usual chores were completed early on Saturday morning. Grey Fann was tackled to the red horse-cart with its large iron-shod wheels. The high turf-creel on the cart was packed with the tools and equipment that were needed – two flat-bottomed wheelbarrows, two *slauns*, two pitchforks, a spade, a shovel, a bottle of paraffin oil to start a fire and, of course, that wicker lunch basket. There was just about enough room for Dad and myself to stand up at the front. The three neighbours would take their bicycles, giving Grey Fann a half-hour headstart.

On arriving at the bog the cart was emptied and Grey Fann was turned loose to graze. While the bog was commonly called the 'mountain', it was in fact a vast area of highland, covered with blanket bog, which had grown over many centuries. Evidence that it was once a forest was seen in the many trunks and stumps of large trees which had been uncovered by turf-cutting. Preserved for centuries in the airless depths of the bog, the bog deal or bog oak was now much sought-after as additional fuel for home fires.

While we waited for our three neighbours to arrive, Dad took his favourite *slaun* and, standing on top of the stripped bank of turf, quietly blessed himself, before beginning to cut out the first of the long wet rectangular sods. The turf was cut in four, sometimes five, horizontal layers or bars, and spread out on the heather in a wide band, to be dried by wind and sun. When our friends arrived, one of them loaded the newly cut sods on the wheelbarrow and spread them in loosely packed formation some distance from the verge of the bank. The other bars would then be spread inside the first lot until the whole upper surface of the bank was covered with the wet sods. As Dad moved slowly backwards, lifting each sod carefully and laying it on the heather at the feet of the spreader, the other two neighbours formed a second team, cutting and spreading the second bar. It was very hard work and soon all four were sweating, though they continued to chat, tell stories and enjoy a few good laughs. My efforts to help were gently but firmly discouraged and by unanimous choice I was put in charge of the catering for the day.

My first duty was to go to the spring-well near the main road for a bucket of water. While I was gone, Dad lit a small fire at the far side of the acre, using some pieces of bog deal, bits of dry turf left lying on the ground from the previous year, and a liberal dousing of the paraffin. It was burning brightly on my return, with a thick column of black smoke rising into the cloudless sky. I filled the big black kettle and balanced it as best I could in the glowing embers. It was hot smokey work but I was determined to give good service to the four men. Dad shouted across to me that I should make them 'a fast cup' now. I watched the kettle intently until a strong jet of steam came out of the spout, even though it was difficult to distinguish the steam from the swirling smoke. I made the tea in the large teapot and, being a little uncertain of the correct amount of tea-leaves to use, I threw in an extra fistful for good measure. Better a little on the strong side than too weak!

I called the men to our picnic site and proudly filled their mugs from the red-hot teapot, my first public appearance as a caterer! As I added some sugar and milk to my own enamel mug, I noticed that the tea had a rather bluish tinge, but dismissed it as being a trick of the sunlight. The men picked up the mugs and raised them to their parched lips for the first welcome mouthful. As I reached for my own first sip of tea, a torrent of curses and swear-words assailed my ears. I looked up to see all four of them spitting. Too late, I drank. Again too late, I tried to spit it out. It was horrible, it was a liquid disaster! Not alone was the tea far too strong, it had the vile taste of paraffin oil. It even had the sharp acrid smell of oily smoke. The men's faces were puckered up in grimaces of distaste as they emptied their mugs in the surrounding heather. I was utterly dejected after all my effort and good intentions. The cursing and spitting subsided and, seeing my look of misery, they began to laugh at my discomfort.

I had watched Mother make tea thousands of times and it was always perfect. What had I done wrong?

'Don't worry,' our neighbour Michael consoled me. 'You'll do much better at lunchtime.' I began to doubt it very much!

Dad turned to me and said, 'Well at least you've learned one thing on the bog today. Whenever you boil a kettle in the open air, always turn the spout straight into the wind and away from the smoke. That's why your tea tasted like poison.'

His advice was good. The lunchtime and evening tea tasted just like tea was supposed to taste, well, almost, and I got no further complaints. By evening, the mountain of food packed by Mother had vanished. I feel that I contributed more than my share to that situation. There is nowhere in the world like the bog for developing a ravenous appetite.

About two weeks later, the wind and sun had dried the exposed sides of the freshly-cut sods into a hard crust. It was time for the turning. After finishing the morning chores, Dad tied a two-prong fork to the crossbar of his bicycle and cycled to the bog. With a deft flick of the fork, he turned each sod upside down, exposing the wet side to the wind and sun.

A few weeks later, on a Saturday, I joined him in the bog to help foot the partially dried sods. This involved standing the sods on their ends in clusters of three or four and balancing one or two other sods across the top of the little pyramid or *grugaun*. It may sound like a very simple task, but it is the most back-breaking of all farmwork because one has to work continuously while bent over at the waist. After an hour of this work, straightening one's back and standing upright can cause twinges of excruciating pain. Experts say that after about four days of footing, the work gets easier and the pains disappear. However, I am in no position to verify such a statement. Surviving day one was an achievement, a feat I had no wish to repeat for at least a week! Not alone did every vertebrae in my back ache individually but my uncalloused schoolroom hands had been chaffed raw from grasping and lifting the rough, abrasive edges of the half-dried sods.

Because of the soft nature of the bog, it was rarely possible to carry a full horse-creel of turf from the bank to the farmyard. Two stages were necessary. In very small loads, the dried turf was put out from the bank to the side of the solid gravelled road. We were among the lucky ones in that Grey Fann could be used in the putting out. Many unfortunate people had to use baskets, which they carried on their backs, or wheelbarrows, or a donkey where the bog was too soft for a horse. At the gravelled road the turf was stacked and clamped in a temporary rick. It was always advisable to transport it home as quickly as possible. In my father's case, however, it was a slow process; two horse-creels a day was the average because of the distance.

Leaving the temporary rick of turf unattended for too long at the side of the road was not recommended. The bog had its predators! There were a few nocturnal visitors who travelled the network of bog roads, stealing a cart load of turf from the temporary ricks and selling it in the town to unsuspecting customers for a pound a load. Those elusive turf robbers were hard to catch and even harder to convict. One victim of numerous raids on his rick, suspected a particular individual and set a trap for him. He marked many of the sods by inserting a horse-shoe nail through the dry crust. The thief was apprehended by the Guards as he tried to sell his stolen load. Later, in court, he was found guilty and given a hefty fine of five pounds or thirty days in jail. A week later he paid the fine at the local Garda barracks. When asked by an inquisitive shopkeeper how he had managed to get the money for the heavy fine, he replied, 'Yerrah, no bother at all. Out of the same rick, sir!'

The time-consuming method of bringing home the turf by horse and cart underwent a dramatic change in the late '40s. An enterprising local man purchased the first lorry in the area and work which had previously taken several weeks to complete could now be done in a day or two. With plenty of neighbours willing to help, three or four lorries of turf could be carried home in one day. There was never any shortage of helpers because riding home on top of the lorry of turf was a great novelty. By driving slowly, the main road through the bog at Mountrivers presented no problem. But the primitive branch roads were never built to take such heavy loads. Travelling on those little roads was a nightmare for both driver and onlookers as the lorry inched its way along the spongy, undulating track, swaying dangerously from side to side, each deep rut presenting a fresh challenge to the skill and the nerve of the driver. Overturning was not unusual, but the safety-conscious driver never allowed anybody to climb on top of the load until they had reached the main road.

Mike Pats was an exception to this rule. He was one of our local characters, always welcome on his *cuaird* because of his wit and endless repertoire of stories. He was a tall, gaunt man with a battered tweed cap perched on the side of his head. A battle-scarred turned-down pipe never seemed to leave the corner of his mouth and was such a permanent feature that he would scarcely be recognised without it. He loved his few pints of stout on Sundays and fair days and was well known for his aversion to exertion. His plot of turf at Mountrivers was some distance up one of the branch roads and on this particular occasion his winter's supply of turf was stacked in a temporary rick at the roadside.

The lorry was hired to carry home Mike Pat's winter fuel and five or six of Mike Pats' neighbours were at hand to fill the lorry. When the turf had reached the top of the high creel of the lorry, Mike Pats climbed up, piling the sods in a large pyramid to ensure that the maximum amount of turf was carried home and that he got maximum value for money. Eventually the driver called a halt to the proceedings and said he would carry no more because he was already overloaded. A long argument ensued as he tried to get Mike Pats to climb down off the load and stay down until they reached the main road. But he refused to budge. Knowing Mike Pats only too well, the worried driver abandoned the argument.

The lorry began to move slowly down the slight incline, inching its way through the deep ruts and swaying from side to side. It lurched dangerously to one side and miraculously recovered, but the top of the load toppled off, landing in the soft bog at the side of the road in a cloud of flying turf dust. The driver stopped immediately and rushed to the side of the lorry. There was no sign of Mike Pats. He had disappeared! Frantically, the driver and the neighbours began digging into the pile of turf which, fortunately, was of a very light, branlike quality. Eventually they uncovered the dust-streaked face of Mike Pats, with the pipe still gripped between his strong teeth.

'Great God almighty, are you dead, Mike?' exclaimed the very worried driver.

'Wisha, I'm not,' said Mike, talking as usual out of the corner of his mouth, 'but I think I'm unconscious!'

CHAPTER 4

A Returned War Hero

ON SMALL FARMS, the amount of land devoted to crops was rarely more than two acres. Year after year, potatoes, cabbage, turnips and other root vegetables were sown in the same gardens. Because of this over-cultivation, fertilisers were needed to sustain a good crop yield. Farmyard manure, euphemistically known as 'top dressing', was scarce, and so local farmers were forced to look for an alternative to supplement the requirements of their fields and gardens. We were fortunate in that we lived within a mile and a half of the sea where an abundance of seaweed was available. Though far from being the ideal fertiliser, its mineral contents certainly promoted growth.

Each spring my father spent at least a week drawing load after load of the wet slippery seaweed from the strand for the potato garden and the meadows. This was usually after the high March spring-tide which deposited large mounds of the weed on the foreshore. It was always a great delight for me to accompany Dad and the horse, Grey Fann, because I loved the strand and the friendly people who eked out a meagre living working there. They had countless stories about the sea and were never too busy to talk to an inquisitive boy who was fascinated by the lore of the strand.

Through riding in the big timber creel with Dad, I came

to know most of the occupants of the houses along the way. They were a poor people, making a very scanty livelihood from fishing in their flimsy currachs, from kelp-burning and from selling pieces of washed-up war wreckage. But they were cheerful and generous, and as we passed by their neat thatched houses on our way to the strand, they shouted greetings to Dad. He had many friends among them. Every time I went with him, one of them was sure to give me a little present of a fistful of dried sea-grass, dillisk, or freshly cooked periwinkles. Many years later, when my father had passed away, I discovered from my friends by the strand that when times were harsh he had often called to one or other of the houses with a couple of buckets of potatoes, a few heads of cabbage, a few bottles of milk, or a horse-creel of turf in winter. They did not forget!

Betsy and Mike lived in a small thatched house beside the strand. They had raised a large family of ten children, all of whom had no option but to leave home and find work in different parts of the world. By the time I began to visit the strand with Dad, Betsy and Mike lived alone, their family scattered.

In appearance, they were a total contrast to each other. Betsy was a big muscular woman, dwarfing Mike who barely reached to her shoulder. Her dark face was set in a perpetual scowl, issuing a warning signal to anybody who might cross her path. She wore a thick woollen headscarf, knotted securely under her chin, and a cross-over apron which partially covered her long black dress. She was a lady not to be trifled with, and all who knew her tried to avoid being the target of her bad temper and sharp tongue. Be it neighbour, friend or relation, nobody escaped a tongue-lashing at some point. It was said that many a fisherman felt the sting of her temper for some transgression, either real or imagined. But though everybody knew her faults and weaknesses, nobody would say a bad word against her.

When Betsy had something to say, she didn't pull punches, and when she spoke in anger, her deep loud voice carried, over a wide area, her opinion of the character, the parenthood and the dubious ancestry of her unfortunate victim. Born into one of the last of the Irish-speaking families from the nearby island, she never forgot her mother-tongue, especially the ancient curses. In a heated argument, her bilingual bad language put even the most hardened fisherman to shame. Her grasp of swear words in English was easily surpassed by her broad range of Irish curses. Among the more mild ones, all of which have long-since faded from the vernacular, were 'Tornac ort' (May thunder and lightning kill you) and 'Colar ort' (May cholera strike you).

It should be said in her favour that she was a very hard worker and a kind and generous neighbour who would give you the shirt off her back but her greatest problem was her furious temper. At some point in her distant past, she had a war of words with the parish priest and, though she probably won that argument too, she refused for years afterwards to go to church. She had very little regard for priests, dismissing them as 'the bloody crowd with the white collars', though she became reconciled with Rome in her final years. In the meantime, several priests had made foolhardy attempts to coerce her into returning to the church, but they usually departed, with ringing ears, much faster than they had arrived.

During a parish Mission, one parish priest decided that the time had come for Betsy to return to the fold. But being a wise and prudent man, well aware of Betsy's reputation, he sent one of the missionaries instead of going himself. Within a matter of minutes after meeting Betsy, the missioner felt he was fighting a losing battle. Knowing the ordinary person's fear of the power of the priests, he retreated to his last line of defence. 'I'm warning you right now, my good woman,' he roared at her, 'if you are not at mass next Sunday, I'll come back again and, with the powers which I possess, I'll turn you into a goat!'

Betsy glared at him with fire in her eyes before replying, 'Well then, me black bucko, if you do that, I'll puck your ass for you in front of me, from here to the chapel gates.'

In contrast, Mike was very mild-mannered and inoffensive. His dress never varied – a peaked *báinín* cap delicately balanced over one ear, a thick hand-knitted polo-necked sweater, or *geansaí*, and heavy hobnailed boots, with the legs of his tweed trousers stuffed into the tops of his woollen socks. His round, cherubic face concealed a sharp, alert mind. Mike was a natural survivor. After a few pints of stout, he became quite garrulous, telling endless stories of his exploits on board a British battleship during World War I. As the pints flowed, he recounted the ever-increasing number of fistfights he had easily won against a variety of British sailors, all of whom were twice his size! Everyone listened intently to his constantly changing stories, though they all believed that Mike had never been in a fistfight in his life. He had enjoyed his four years in the British navy and always addressed everybody as 'Sailor'. His 'four glorious years in the navy, fighting for the rights of small nations', had actually been spent ashore working in the navy dockyard or, as Betsy so succinctly phrased it during a squabble, 'He spent four years doing nothing in Southampton and then the hoor tried to spend the best part of the next twenty years in bed, to recover from his exertions.'

At the end of the Great War, Mike returned to Betsy and their large family. But he came back to a local economy that suffered deep depression in the post-war period. The War of Independence, better known as the 'Black-and-Tan War', was still on, only to be followed by the Civil War. The local fishing fleet had all but vanished because the small fish-salting factory at the pier had closed through lack of demand. The cheap importation of iodine-bearing minerals from Chile to Glasgow ended the burning of kelp, except for a brief revival during World War II. Mike and his fellow fishermen lived from day to day, happy just to survive. Their main diet was fish, either fresh, salted or smoked, while their only income came from selling fresh fish. They travelled far inland in their donkeys and carts, selling fresh mackerel to housewives for sixpence a dozen.

Mike found it very difficult to make ends meet. His pleasures were few, perhaps the occasional pint of stout and, when he had the money, a half-quarter – two ounces of common stout tobacco. This he shared with Betsy. She liked a quiet smoke at night when the children were gone to bed. She kept a clay pipe hidden on top of the dresser so that the children or the neighbours would not find out about her little pleasure.

Mike hated both the hard work and the poverty and often wished he was back with the navy. Many of his friends and neighbours had also been in the Great War, though several had suffered serious injuries, especially those who had served in the army. Some had come home on crutches or in wheelchairs while others had lost an eye or a limb, or suffered respiratory problems as a result of mustard gas. Each one of the war-wounded was now in receipt of a British army or navy pension. With this they were able to provide for their families and had the security of a guaranteed monthly cheque. Some of them were able to engage in light work on the strand to supplement their small income.

Mike felt a little envious of the easy money his friends were getting. But he had returned unscathed from the war and was not entitled to a disability pension. If only he had received some small injury, preferably of the painless variety. At the funeral of another war veteran, he met a few of his old comrades and availed of the opportunity to probe every possible avenue through which he could claim a disability pension. But it was hopeless! Over a couple of pints in the local pub, he listened to the other ex-servicemen as they spoke sadly about some of their friends who had seen the horrors of war at close range and were now shell-shocked, suffering from badly shattered nerves, even to the point of mild insanity. Mike's agile mind grasped at a straw. He casually enquired about the symptoms, the medical examinations and, of course, the size of the pension.

He returned home to Betsy, deep in thought, with the

germ of a plan developing in his nimble mind. Burdened with the problems of surviving in those harsh times, Betsy became a willing co-conspirator. They got a young local girl who was 'good at writing' to write to the navy pensions office. They received a prompt reply together with two railway tickets, inviting Mike to attend an interview and a medical examination.

Arriving at the appointed time, Betsy and Mike were confronted by an inspector and a doctor. Betsy did all the talking while Mike, with a well-rehearsed vacant expression on his face and his lips moving in silent conversation, appeared to have no interest in the discussion. On being questioned, Betsy explained the three or four year delay in making their application. 'Wisha, sir, I didn't want to be bothering you,' she explained in a sorrowful voice. 'Sure, I thought that you'd have to have lost a leg or an arm or an eye before you could get a pension. Poor Mike can't do any work at all. I have to keep an eye on him the whole time.'

She paused for a moment before continuing, 'But sure he's no trouble at all. He's just like a big child.' She had to be careful that the disability did not appear to be too severe and that she was quite capable of caring for him; otherwise they might send him to an institution and that would ruin everything. Once or twice during the interview Mike tugged at Betsy's black shawl and said in a soft, childlike voice, 'Mamma, I want to go home and play with the lads!'

The inspector and doctor looked at each other and nodded sympathetically, obviously deeply moved by the love, the loyalty and the bravery of this hard-working woman who stood by her man through thick and thin. Without further ado, they awarded Mike a disability pension. There would be an annual visit from the inspector to check for any signs of an improvement in his condition.

On arriving back at the local station, the happy couple marched side by side to the nearby pub where they celebrated with a few glasses of stout in the snug – a small cubicle reserved for female customers; women at that time never drank in public and would not be served at the public bar. For Mike and Betsy, it was a farewell to hardship. Now they were assured of a small weekly cheque which would be sufficient for their basic needs. In their uncomplicated logic, they saw nothing morally wrong in their actions. Mike felt that he had assisted the navy with four years of loyal service and now it was the turn of the navy to assist him. Survival was their main concern and they were overjoyed that they had found a way of keeping the wolf from the door.

The navy pension arrived each Thursday. About a year later, they received a letter from the inspector advising them of the date and time of his first visit. At the appointed time, Mike was seen running up and down in front of the house playing 'bowley', rolling the spokeless wheel of an old bicycle with a piece of stick. The inspector spoke to Betsy outside the front door while Mike waved a greeting to him as he continued to play his game, balancing the rolling wheel with the stick. The inspector shook his head sadly and left, convinced that Mike's disability was as bad as ever.

After a few years playing this particular game, Mike

decided that a change of act was called for, especially since he found that playing bowley was utterly exhausting. As the inspector approached the house on the next annual visit, Mike stood on a timber chair by the fire and, crouching down on his heels, he flapped his elbows repeatedly, hoarsely squawking 'Quack! Quack! Quack!'

The inspector looked at him and muttered, 'Oh dear, oh dear, I think it's worse he's getting. Does he believe he's a duck?'

Betsy nodded and grunted under her breath, 'An old drake would be more like it!' Betsy was unhappy with the new act and felt that they were over-doing it a little. After long deliberation during the following months, Mike thought of a plan, a plan which was brilliant in its simplicity and free from unwelcome exertion.

On the inspector's next visit, Betsy greeted him in the little gravelled yard at the front of the house. 'And where is your good husband on this lovely day?' he asked.

'Wisha, he's fishing away for himself at the back of the house,' Betsy replied.

'Good gracious me, he's cured,' exclaimed the inspector in delight as he dashed around the gable end of the house. Mike was sitting on a *súgán* chair close to the back door, holding a short piece of a stick from which dangled three or four feet of twine and a bent safety-pin. In front of him was a large galvanised wash-tub, filled with water.

'And how are we feeling today, Michael?' the inspector asked brightly.

Mike turned sharply towards him and whispered urgently, with a finger to his lips, 'Shhh ... Will you shush your mouth, you eejit? Can't you see that they're biting mad today. We'll have a fine feed of fresh fish for our supper.'

The inspector turned sadly away. He visited Mike for a number of years after that. Each time Mike was fishing. Eventually it was decided that Mike's disability was 'stable but incurable', with no further need for an annual inspection, though the good inspector warned Betsy that if Mike's condition deteriorated and she needed further assistance, she should write to him immediately. With a well-practised look of resigned suffering, Betsy agreed!

For years afterwards, Mike kept his fishing tackle hanging on a nail outside the back door, ready at all times for a surprise inspection. But there was none. And the life-saving cheque still arrived in the post each Thursday.

CHAPTER 5

A Match Made in Lisdoonvarna

ABOUT A MILE from our house a hard-working couple lived on their thirty-acre farm. Pat Tom and Mary were acknowledged as good, honest people and great neighbours. Their four children had grown up, two living away from home, Joe in the civil service in Dublin and Maura nursing in a hospital in London. The older son Paddy, the heir-apparent to the land, and his slightly younger sister Kitty, lived at home with Pat Tom and Mary. Paddy had been doing a strong line with a neighbour, Nancy, since schooldays but needed a little encouragement to proceed further, even though he was fast approaching his mid-thirties. Both families were very much in favour of a marriage but the easy-going lad was in no particular hurry to rush into the responsibilities of marriage.

Eventually Paddy summoned up the courage to take the vital step. Arrangements were quickly made, with the wedding to take place when all the farm work was completed, about the first week in November. Nancy would bring with her a welcome dowry of four hundred pounds which ensured that Kitty could now marry into an even bigger farm than was originally anticipated. An incoming dowry was not considered disposable income but was re-used as the 'fortune' of another son or daughter when they got married and moved into some other farmer's place. Thus a fortune could be traced, moving from one farm to another, over several generations. But while Paddy's forthcoming marriage solved one problem, it created another. Two women in the same kitchen could occasionally cause problems, but three would certainly invite disaster! Efforts had to be made to get Kitty happily married into some farmer's place, the bigger the better, as soon as was reasonably possible. Kitty was a quiet, pleasant girl and was very shy. Possibly because of her strict parents, she never had a steady boyfriend.

Some initial approaches to making a suitable match for her had been undertaken discreetly by a few close relatives, but so far nothing positive had emerged. Neither Pat Tom nor Mary wanted it to be public knowledge that they were husband-hunting for Kitty. It would hurt their family pride if the neighbours thought that they had become desperate. But now, after several discussions, Pat Tom and Mary decided that drastic measures were called for. A week's holiday in Lisdoonvarna could be the answer. But it would have to appear to the neighbours to be a casual visit and have no connection whatsoever with Kitty's protracted single status. It was a major decision that demanded good planning, shrewdness and initiative. Keeping the neighbours in the dark was most important. Even though it was only early May, Mary took out her pen and paper and wrote to a guesthouse in Lisdoonvarna, making reservations for the second week in September for Pat Tom.

It must be stated at this point that going on holidays was an almost unheard-of luxury in our area along the west coast. Money was still a constant problem for people and to spend it on a holiday was an extravagance few could afford. There were some exceptions but they were very rare. The priests of the parish usually took a few weeks off from parish work to visit their family homes in distant east Clare or Tipperary where, it was rumoured with good authority, they took off their clerical collars and helped with the saving of the hay and other farm work just like ordinary people! But in general the only people who took real holidays were those who had 'permanent pensionable government jobs', such as the master and his family who, each year, went to Salthill, Tramore or Kerry for two weeks, coming back looking very refreshed and with nice sun-tans. It should come as no surprise that it was the ambition of every local farmer to get as many as possible of his family on the government payroll! It guaranteed security, status, money and annual holidays, all without having to dirty one's hands.

But it was almost unthinkable for any of the locals to take a week's holiday. It would make them helpless targets for slagging and sarcastic jokes. Some would even consider it a sign of weakness. It was as though the rare few who indulged in a holiday were in some way stepping beyond the limits of acceptable behaviour and developing notions of bigness far above their station in life. At best, taking a holiday would elicit begrudging remarks such as: 'Wisha, 'tis well for him that he couldn't find enough work to do at home!' However, in our area, a few elderly farmers who had grown-up sons working on the farm made the annual pilgrimage for a week or two each September to Lisdoonvarna, the spa, about twenty miles away. Here they would meet old acquaintances and, in that town famous for its matchmaking, would be on the look-out for a suitable match for one of their sons or daughters.

About two weeks before his impending holiday, Pat Tom went on *cuaird* as usual to a neighbour's house where most of the local farmers gathered around the fire to discuss the events of the day and, of course, collect some of the local gossip. Pat Tom sat waiting for his opportunity to break the news. The strategy devised by Mary and himself was that the long-planned week in Lisdoonvarna had to appear to the neighbours to be a spur-of-the-moment medical decision in which he would be the unwilling victim. Any hint that he was looking forward to his week's holiday could damage his image as a hardworking farmer and those bucko's sitting around the fire could easily begin looking for ulterior motives for his trip to the spa!

The conversation around the fire skipped from one subject to another until it came to rest on a very popular country topic, aches, pains and ailments. Pat Tom instantly seized the opportunity. As though it was an afterthought, he casually remarked, 'Speaking of ailments, ever since I got a bad wettin' a couple of years ago, I've been pestered with rheumatism in that right hip.'

He moved gingerly in the *súgán* chair to emphasise his discomfort before continuing, 'Whether it's a sign of rain or not, I don't know, but it's acting up fierce with the last week or so. 'Twas only this morning that Mary was at me again to go up to the sulphur baths in Lisdoonvarna for a week. They say they're very good, but sure 'tis too late now in the year to be trying to book into one of the guesthouses. Nothing would do Mary but to write this morning to a couple of the places in the spa even though I told her 'twas a waste of time and anyway there's still far too much work to be done at home.'

His listeners sagely nodded their heads at his tale of troubles, were very sympathetic to his newly announced ailment and fully understood his unwillingness to go to the spa, leaving so many unfinished jobs at home!

When it was time to go home, he visibly grimaced with the effort to stand up and straighten his right leg. His neighbours asked if he could manage to walk home but he assured them, 'Once the leg softens out I'll be fine.' He left for home, happy in the belief that he had successfully completed the hardest part of his mission, that of fooling the neighbours. Or so he thought. His smugness would have vanished like a puff of smoke if he could hear the conversation around the fire after his departure. His carefully woven veil of aches and pains was transparent to his listeners. The well-rehearsed story was as familiar to those shrewd farmers as the words of a favourite old song. Speculating on Pat Tom's next move, they gleefully awaited Act Two of the charade.

Two or three nights before his long-awaited crusade to the spa, Pat Tom again went on *cuaird* to join his neighbours. After almost an hour of desultory conversation, one of the neighbours around the fire decided to set the ball rolling by asking Pat Tom if the rheumatism was still bothering him. It was an ideal opening for Pat Tom and he grabbed the bait. 'Well, bad luck to it, but 'tis worse it's after getting,' Pat Tom replied, warming to his well-rehearsed lines. 'Tis funny that you mentioned it but didn't Mary get a letter from Miss White's in Lisdoonvarna only this morning that she was after getting a sudden cancellation and that she could fix me up for a week or so, starting the day after tomorrow.'

Everybody around the fire congratulated him on his apparent good fortune. But Pat Tom gave the impression that he was rather unhappy with the sudden turn of events. 'The last thing I want to do is go up to the spa for a full week and I having a pile of work to do. But I won't get a minute's peace from Mary unless I go. I've a good mind to make her write back tomorrow and cancel it.'

A chorus of disapproval rose from around the blazing turf fire. While they were sympathetic to the sentiments he expressed, it was overwhelmingly decided that Mary had his best interests at heart, that the sulphur baths would do him the world of good and that he would come home a new man. After much grumbling, he allowed them to persuade him to go to the spa. He walked home that night with a spring in his step, convinced that he had hoodwinked them completely.

At last the fateful morning arrived. Pat Tom was attired in his Sunday best. His navy-blue serge suit, still reeking of the pungent smell of camphor balls, was neatly pressed and his starch-stiffened shirt and collar were gleaming white. Mary insisted that he wear the large, wide, flower-patterned silk tie that had arrived the previous Christmas in a parcel from his sister in America. His beloved tweed peaked cap was discarded and was replaced by a grey felt hat with a turned-down brim which had spent most of its long life inside an old pillowcase on top of the wardrobe. Mary was quite satisfied with her well turned-out husband. He looked, in her view, like a prosperous farmer!

The previous night, Mary had packed his suitcase, or his portmanteau as she preferred to call it. Showing a total lack of confidence in the two flimsy snap-locks, Pat Tom had ensured against their disintegration and any attempted larceny, by tying the suitcase around the middle with several coils of strong cord. Inside the fortified suitcase, Mary had packed a few shirts with detached white collars wrapped in tissue paper, a spare pair of longjohns, a vest, socks, a half-pound of tea and a pound of sugar which were still rationed, his cut-throat razor together with some red and white striped flannelette pyjamas. Pat Tom hated pyjamas. He saw no logic whatsoever in 'dressing up to go to bed'.

The previous year he had stayed overnight in Limerick for the wedding of his niece and, of course, had to wear the pyjamas for the sake of appearances. He found them unreasonably hot and uncomfortable and felt very overdressed, 'looking like a right eejit in convict stripes!' As Mary placed them in the suitcase, he promised himself that if he had a room to himself in Lisdoonvarna, there would be no pyjamas. The thought suddenly occurred to him that he would crumple them in an untidy ball at the end of his stay and that Mary would never know the difference.

Mary drove him in the pony and trap to Kilmurry station. Throwing the reins over the pony's head and tying it to the gate leading to the platform, they walked to

John the Station Master's office where Pat Tom bought a return ticket to Ennistymon, the nearest station to Lisdoonvarna. They were in plenty of time. John told them that the west Clare train had just left Doonbeg and would not reach Kilmurry for another fifteen minutes. They moved to the end of the gravelled platform, well beyond earshot of the curious onlookers. There they engaged in animated conversation, though this may be considered a poor description because it seemed that Mary did all the talking while Pat Tom did all the listening.

'Last minute instructions, no doubt, before they throw in the ball,' quipped one of the watching locals who would later update the neighbours on developments.

In less than an hour the train huffed and puffed its way into Ennistymon station. Near the exit gate, Robbie the hackney-driver advertised his services in a loud voice, 'Hackney car for the spa'. Pat Tom and two elderly couples piled into the roomy but ancient vehicle, each gladly paying the two-shilling fare for the nine-mile journey to Lisdoonvarna.

The road from Ennistymon to the spa wound its way uphill, climbing steadily from a little above sea-level to the heart of the Burren plateau. Robbie was a great conversationalist after a lifetime spent transporting customers around north Clare, first with horse and sidecar and now with his pride and joy, a gleaming Armstrong-Siddley. By the time they reached the creamery on the edge of the town, he had his five passengers talking to each other and by the time they reached Kilshanny, the halfway point, they were all like old friends. They were soon talking freely about their farms and their families at home.

Pat Tom, when it came to his turn to speak, decided that the two couples in the car with him were honest decent people and could well prove to be good ambassadors for his mission. Mary and himself had discussed how the subject of a match for Kitty should be approached. Even if his new friends turned out to be of little use to his quest, he would at least have some practice at telling his story!

He began by assuring them that he was blessed by God with a healthy, happy family and a good piece of land. He explained that his son, 'the boy for the place', had been keeping company with a neighbour's daughter for a few years and was very anxious to get married towards the end of the year. As though it was an afterthought, he casually mentioned that his daughter Kitty still lived at home with them.

'A great girl,' Pat Tom expanded. 'A mighty worker! She can turn her hand to anything! She's very quiet and gentle, and was never sick a day in her life. She seems to be in no hurry to get married, though she has had plenty of boyfriends. But to tell you the truth, Mary and myself are getting on a bit and we'd love to see her settled down, even though we'd hate to lose her. She'd make a great wife for some respectable young farmer and, faith, I'd see to it that she wouldn't be going empty-handed into a good farm. She'd have a nice bit of money going with her!'

His new friends listened attentively, recognising immediately the unspoken purpose of Pat Tom's visit to Lisdoonvarna. The intrigue of matchmaking with its protracted wheeling-and-dealing had a mass appeal among the rural population of Ireland. It was most people's dream to play a leading role in making a successful match. Both couples in the car recognised the opportunity of enhancing their visit to the spa with the prospect of discovering a suitable husband for the fair Kitty.

Entering into the spirit of the intrigue, one of the men said to Pat Tom, 'It was God brought us together in this motor-car because it could easily happen that we might hear of the perfect match for your fine daughter.'

Pat Tom thanked him, already feeling more confident! They reached Lisdoonvarna, passing the spa wells and the bathhouse on their way up the hill to the centre of the town. Robbie drove them to the northern end of the main street, where they were delighted to discover that they were booked into adjoining guesthouses, quite close to the magnificent limestone parish church.

After enjoying a good lunch, Pat Tom walked back down the street, familiarising himself with the location of the different hotels where the well-off farmers stayed. He felt a little guilty walking around the town, dressed up in his Sunday clothes, on a sunny work day. However, he consoled himself with the thought that what he was doing in Lisdoonvarna was also very important work. That night and for several nights afterwards, he visited each of the hotels, striking up a conversation with different farmers in the bars. After a bottle or two of stout, he always managed to bring the topic of conversation around to the subject of families, repeating his now well-rehearsed story.

After two nights of such activity, he decided that phase one of his campaign was completed. He would now await results. The marital grapevine in that matchmaking capital was exceptionally strong. To continue repeating his story would be to appear over anxious and would weaken his bargaining position.

He continued to visit the hotel bars, having a glass of stout in each one, thereby making himself available should anybody be looking for him. The seeds had been sown and now he awaited the harvest! A few inquisitive people asked him the exact size of his daughter's dowry but he was not willing to divulge any details until a positive approach was made. He knew he would have up to four hundred pounds to offer as a fortune but would, if the proper occasion presented itself, offer a dowry of three hundred pounds, giving himself plenty of room to increase it gradually to his upper limit. That was the unwritten code of behaviour in such circumstances.

Two further days of inactivity followed. Pat Tom had to admit to himself that he was enjoying his first holiday. The days had been spent with some of his new friends, walking around the tree-shrouded sulphur wells and the baths, He would now be able to speak with authority about the spa the next time he went on his *cuaird* at home. He even got a large bottle of sulphur water to take on *cuaird* with him, for authenticity. He had tried, with limited success, to drink a glass of the water, but had avoided the bathhouses. Depending on the success or failure of his efforts to find a husband for Kitty, his alleged bad dose of rheumatism would either be completely cured or else might have to go into temporary remission until the following September.

On the third day of his long wait, Pat Tom was having his evening meal when one of the couples who had travelled with him in Robbie's hackney called to see him.

After a few minutes' pleasant conversation, the husband said, 'There's a friend of mine up the street at the Imperial that I'd like you to meet.'

The three of them walked up to the hotel and made their way to the bar. Pat Tom was introduced to the stranger, Seán, a big florid friendly farmer to whom Pat Tom took an instant liking. The helpful couple ordered the first round of drinks, three bottles of stout and a small port. They retired to one of the snugs at the side of the bar where there was much more privacy. By the time the second round of drinks arrived, the conversation had warmed a little as the invisible barriers of shyness and wariness gradually disappeared. Within a half-hour, Pat Tom and Seán were chatting about cattle, hay and tillage like they were old friends. The couple discreetly excused themselves on some pretext or other and left the two men to discuss their own affairs. The friendly conversation between them indicated that no intermediary was required!

Pat Tom was enjoying the chat so much that he actually forgot his main objective in coming to Lisdoonvarna. It was only when he began to tell Seán about his family at home that he lapsed into his oft repeated story.

'Well, Pat Tom, isn't that a mighty strange coincidence,' said Seán. 'We have almost the same kind of predicament in my house. My son at home, Michael, a fine, upright, sober young man, seems to have no notion at all of settling down. He's very shy when it comes to women. 'Tis he will be getting the place because my younger son is in for a priest and sure the only daughter I have is just a child of twenty-three yet.'

He fell silent for a moment, looking into his half-empty

glass of stout. 'Well,' he continued as though talking to himself, 'Wouldn't it beat the devil and Dan Reilly if your daughter and my son ever met and made a match of it? 'Twould ease our minds a lot to know that either of them wouldn't be alone in the world when it's time for us to pass on.'

Pat Tom was inwardly delighted with the sudden turn of events, He was glad now that he had done things on his own rather than approach any of the well-known matchmakers in the town. If he had been looking for a wife for his son Paddy he would have no objection to engaging a matchmaker to help but, when it came to his daughter, somehow or other it did not seem proper! By now his mind was racing at high speed. He assessed the facts he had gathered from the conversation so far – Seán had a good-sized farm with ten cows and a flock of sheep, a slated house on the main road to Ennis and only a couple of miles from Ennistymon and, for icing on the cake, a future priest in the family. 'Twas surely a message straight from heaven! he thought to himself.

'As sure as I'm sitting here, Seán,' Pat Tom replied, 'it didn't strike me until now, but what you say is true. They seem to be a perfect match for each other and 'twould be a mortal sin to keep them apart.'

He paused for a moment as Seán nodded his head in agreement. Pat Tom continued, 'Mary and myself would be fierce lonesome to see her go out from under our roof but sure 'tis her happiness we have to think about. And she wouldn't be leaving with one hand as long as the other either! She has a fine fortune of three hundred pounds put aside for her, but if she met a real nice young man, I wouldn't see her short. I'd throw another hundred pounds on top of that because she is such a great girl.' Pat Tom had played his trump card! They sat silently for a few moments, each busy with his own thoughts.

Eventually Seán broke the silence. 'Do you think there's any way, Pat Tom,' he ventured, 'that we could give them a bit of a push in the right direction and who knows what might come out of it?'

Pat Tom knew immediately that an unspoken initial agreement had been reached on a match, though there were many more steps to be taken before reaching the foot of the altar. 'We'll think of a way, Seán, we'll think of a way,' said Pat Tom as he solemnly shook hands with Seán across the small table.

Great discretion was now required to blind both sets of neighbours to any hint of a made match. After further discussion it was agreed that Pat Tom, Mary and Kitty would 'accidentally' meet Seán, his wife and Michael at the Queen's Hotel in Ennis a week later, where they could all get to know each other better and have a good chat.

It was becoming more fashionable now for the future bride and groom to meet and get to know each other before the marriage ceremony. It had even come to the point where either of the future partners could refuse to proceed further with marriage plans on such grounds as instant dislike to each other or some trivial personality clash! 'Far different from our day, Pat Tom,' Seán remarked a little sadly. 'These young ones are all getting notions of their own instead of listening to us that know what's best for them.'

Pat Tom replied, 'Wisha, Seán, maybe it isn't such a bad

idea at all. In our day, more often than not, we married the land and hoped for the best in the partner. 'Twas often two people met for the first time on the steps of the altar.'

Pat Tom returned from Lisdoonvarna a happy man. Mary was delighted with the good news, though Kitty appeared less elated and looked apprehensive. On the following night, Pat Tom went on his *cuaird*. He was the centre of attraction as he extoled the virtues of Lisdoon-varna, the great rest he had, the good food and the grand people he met from all over the country. They all sampled, with varying degrees of enthusiasm, the bottle of sulphur water he had brought with him. And the baths? By the second day, he told them, he could feel the healing quali-ties of the baths improving the pains in his leg and by the end of the week, 'the blasted rheumatism had disap-peared completely, thanks be to God and his blessed mother.' They were delighted at his miraculous cure!

After he had left for home, one of his listeners quipped, 'Be japers, Pat Tom must have strick oil at the spa. Kitty must be on her way to the altar!'

On the appointed Saturday, Pat Tom, Mary and Kitty quietly boarded the train for the crucial meeting with Seán and his family at the Queen's Hotel. After passing En-nistymon station, they had the small compartment to themselves. Mary had already had several long private discussions with Kitty on matters of marriage and it was time now to give a few directions to Pat Tom as to his general behaviour and his good manners.

'Now, Pat Tom,' she began, 'We have to make a good impression on these people and I don't want you acting like a country cawbogue, do you hear me? Keep that smelly old pipe of yours out of your mouth and don't start talking about snagging turnips, or spreading manure or cows calving or bulls or any of your dirty stories that you seem to think are very funny. And whatever you do, don't mention that there was a touch of consumption in your Aunt Bridget's family, even though it didn't come from your side, God preserve us!'

She paused for breath and to allow him time to absorb her instructions, before continuing, 'And above all, watch your language! I want to hear no swearing or taking the holy name. I'll tell you one thing, Pat Tom, if I hear as much as one "Be Jaysus" out of you for the rest of the day, by Christ I'll flatten you on the way home. And don't start singing "Nancy Hogan's Goose" after a couple of bottles of porter. Act the gentleman for one day, for the sake of your daughter. I'll be keeping a strict eye on you!' Pat Tom accepted all the advice in silence and wondered why he had not stayed at home.

From the station in Ennis, they walked to the hotel at the other side of the town. Seán, his wife and Michael were already there, having driven the mere thirteen miles to town in the horse and trap. The first five or ten minutes were tense, everyone was very reserved and polite as each family sized up the other. Slowly the ice melted and soon both sets of parents were engaged in friendly animated conversation.

Michael and Kitty stole furtive glances at each other across the low table, now laden with a round of drinks. Kitty's fears vanished as she looked at Michael's dark curly hair and his honest open face. She liked him immediately. He was everything she hoped for! And Michael felt instantly attracted to Kitty. He liked the way her good sense of humour was reflected in her big blue eyes. Shyly, at first, they spoke a few words to each other during the rare lulls in their parents' conversation. After an hour, they were all like old friends, chatting about a variety of subjects. They talked about everything except the subject of a match between Kitty and Michael. It would be a breach of good manners to discuss it at this getting-to-know-you meeting. That would be thrashed out at the next stage of the proceedings.

Following accepted protocol, Seán invited Pat Tom and Mary to visit his home on the following Saturday. This signalled to Pat Tom and Mary that Kitty's marriage to Michael was provisionally acceptable and that they would now proceed to the next step. Going home on the train, they had a long chat about the meeting with Seán's family and were delighted to have met such lovely people. Kitty was very shy in discussing her opinion of Michael but both Pat Tom and Mary had read the signs and knew that she liked him and was attracted to him. At least, it was a great start!

CHAPTER 6

Sealed with a Handshake

THE NEGOTIATIONS INVOLVED in the making of a match often demanded a high degree of skill and great bargaining ability. Some were protracted, mediators and ambassadors scurrying back and forth between the two parties with proposals and counter-proposals until eventually a complex agreement was reached. These were the extreme cases, in total contrast to the low-profile, amicable discussions between Pat Tom and Seán. But a breakdown in negotiations at the final stages of the making of a match was considered a stain on the good names of each of the parties involved. It was taken to indicate the presence of a variety of vices – greed, avarice, some mental or physical handicap in either the prospective bride or groom, or just plain thickness in one or other of the families. Greater than usual secrecy was needed in getting over the final hurdle in the matchmaking stakes.

Because another train journey would attract too much unwelcome attention, Pat Tom and Mary decided to travel the sixteen miles to Seán's house in the pony and trap. Some preparations were made, mostly of the cosmetic variety. Mary pushed the trap from the shelter of the lean-to shed at the gable of the cowshed and scrubbed the bodywork and shafts with soap and water until they gleamed. Pat Tom, in the meantime, polished the black leather trap-harness with a lump of fat bacon and buffed it with an old pair of knitted woollen stockings until it was shining. The thin carpet of straw was removed from the floor, or well, of the trap and replaced with a piece of an old mat which Mary cut to shape. The image of a well-to-do farmer must be maintained!

On returning from the creamery on the Saturday morning, Pat Tom tackled the pony to the refurbished trap and, wearing their Sunday clothes, he and Mary set off on their long journey. The fact that Pat Tom wore his old tweed working cap, perched as usual on the side of his head, and that Mary wore a headscarf knotted loosely under her chin, was intended to give the impression that they were only going into the local town to do the messages. But, unseen by their neighbours, a white calico bag lay on the floor of the trap, well concealed by the plaid tasselled rug. In the bag was Pat Tom's fedora hat and Mary's new wide-brimmed blue hat with a large feather on one side and a long mother-of-pearl hatpin on the other. They would change their headgear before reaching Seán's house and hide the cap, scarf and white bag under one of the cushions in the trap.

This visit by the parents of the incoming marriage partner to a farm was of crucial importance, a make-or-break situation in many cases. Traditionally it was known as 'walking the land'. For both sets of parents no exaggeration, bluffing or window-dressing was possible beyond this point. It was a day for hard facts when final agreements would be reached, with each of the parents trying to ensure the future welfare and security of their offspring. Every field in the farm was walked to inspect both quality and quantity. Cows and other farm animals were counted and their condition taken into account. It has been said that there were instances where a few cows and even a few fields were borrowed for the day to enhance the prospects of a desirable match. Fortunately such happenings were rare and were seldom successful. Once walking the land was completed and deemed satisfactory, the matter of the dowry was discussed and agreed on. Many stories were told of hours spent bargaining, haggling and splitting the difference on the question of the dowry before a final figure was reached. Once that matter was settled, all that remained was to agree on a convenient date for 'drawing up the writings' and to fix a date for the wedding.

The drawing up the writings involved signing a legal document, a marriage agreement, drawn up by a solicitor, to protect the rights of all the parties concerned. It was usually a three or four page standard legal document, couched in quaint legal phrases with adequate blank spaces provided for the insertion of additional clauses or for agreed variations in existing ones.

It was only when a son was about to get married that a father would grudgingly relinquish ownership of the farm. On the other side, no sensible father would allow his daughter bring a dowry to a marriage unless her new husband was the full owner of the property. In turn, the welfare of the newly retired parents was protected. While in practice the parents and the newly weds might work together in perfect harmony, provision was made in the writings for the parents to retain use of part of the house, usually the big inside room at one end of the house, as their private domain for the rest of their lives. They were also entitled to free use of the kitchen fireplace for all their cooking needs, together with free turf for the small grate in their room and, of course, free vegetables and milk. In most cases, the provisions of the writings were never invoked. But there were instances where friction, very often in the kitchen between mother and daughter-in-law, made life unbearable for either or both parties. In such unfortunate cases, the protection of the writings proved invaluable.

Following the directions given them, Pat Tom and Mary had no trouble finding Seán's house. As they drew near to the house, Mary cast a knowledgeable eye over the well laid-out fields and expressed her satisfaction. This was her only chance to make an assessment of the quality of the land because walking the land was left entirely to the men. It would be considered unladylike and indelicate for a woman to become involved in such matters!

They were given a royal welcome. The pony was untackled and turned loose into the small, lush, green paddock beside the house. Within a short time of their arrival, they were all sitting around the table, enjoying a dinner of roast chicken with all the trimmings, followed by tea and sweet cake. Mary insisted on helping with the wash-up while the two men sat by the fire, smoking their pipes and enjoying their chat. Michael and his younger sister kept a little in the background, leaving centrestage to the two sets of parents.

After about an hour, Seán invited Pat Tom to go out to have a look at a new cow he had bought recently. There was no direct mention of walking the land. After admiring the new cow and putting a 'God bless' on the rest of the herd, Pat Tom walked along beside Seán. 'Wisha, Pat Tom,' said Seán, 'we may as well go for a stroll back through the fields for a bit and leave the women to themselves in the kitchen.'

Pat Tom liked both the farm and its owners very much and said to himself that his Kitty 'was blessed from heaven to be marrying into such a fine place and such lovely people.'

As they approached the house on their way back from their walk, Seán stopped for a moment. 'By the way, Pat Tom,' he said, 'herself and myself were talking and, if it's all right with yourself and Mary, we both agreed that Kitty's fortune is more than generous. She's a grand girl, Pat Tom, and you needn't worry, we'll love her like she was our own daughter.'

The two men looked each other in the eye and silently shook hands. 'I think,' said Pat Tom, 'we'll go inside and try and talk those two women round to our way of thinking. Unless they get too contrary altogether, we'll fix a day for drawing up the writings and then leave the wedding plans to them. They're the best for that sort of thing.'

On arriving back in the kitchen, they discovered that the two mothers had anticipated their decision and had become the best of friends. They seemed to have regained their girlish youth as they busied themselves making plans for the wedding. 'Begorrah, Seán,' said Pat Tom, 'it looks as if our good ladies didn't even bother waiting for the two of us before they started planning and scheming between themselves.'

Seán smiled ruefully. 'I'll say one thing for them, Pat Tom, they don't be dancing around the bush like the two of us, but they get right to the point and no cod-acting!'

The afternoon passed far too quickly for guests and hosts. Finally, looking up at the big clock hanging over the open fireplace, Pat Tom said, 'Great God, Mary, we'd better tackle up the pony and hit for the west, the way we'll be home with the daylight. We'd never live it down if a civic guard caught us with no light in the trap.'

The women had already decided that, with Mary's son getting married in early November and with the approach of the season of advent, the most suitable date for the wedding of Kitty and Michael was the end of January. The writings would be drawn up shortly after New Year's Day and the wedding would be three weeks later. That would give plenty of time for Paddy's new wife to settle down. It would also mean that Kitty had lots of time to purchase her trousseau, or as Pat Tom termed it, her 'fol-de-rols'. It was settled. Michael was delighted with the outcome and he felt that Kitty would also be very pleased. Both of them had explicit trust in the wisdom and judgement of their parents.

As the pony trotted homeward into the fading October sunset, Pat Tom was feeling very pleased and happy and knew that God had been good to himself and his family. But the transformation in Mary was astonishing! She filled the trap with happy chatter as they drove along. Pat Tom was a little taken aback at the change. It seemed as though a great weight had been lifted from her shoulders. For thirty-five years she had worried and prayed, slaved and scrounged for her children. And now the last of them was about to embark on a good life, on a good farm and with a good husband and kind in-laws. It was worth all the agony and the pain. She was happy. Pat Tom thought she looked nearly twenty years younger as she talked to him about the great chat she had had with Seán's wife. The lines of care and worry, yes, even the lines of bitterness seemed to have faded from her face.

She stopped suddenly and looked across the trap at Pat Tom. 'You know what, Pat Tom,' she said, 'You and I have had our share of ups and downs. There were times when you could get as thick as a ditch and I suppose there were times when I was a bit sharp too, a bit hard on you. We've had our hard times but we always managed to get through them, thank God. But it was above in Seán's house that it struck me – didn't we do all right, the two of us, with our four children.'

She paused for a moment before continuing. 'There's young Paddy at home, getting married soon to a grand little girl from down the road, that we've known since she was a child. There's Joe above in Dublin in the civil service and doing well for himself in a lovely cushy job. There's Maura, a nursing sister in that big hospital over in London, and now there's Kitty all fixed up to get married into a fine place and a fine hunk of a man. Do you know what, Pat Tom, 'tis blest we are, pure blest!'

Pat Tom nodded his head in agreement, beginning to see Mary in a new light. Suddenly he too was filled with happiness and satisfaction at the thought that like the young birds at the end of the summer, his family were now fully feathered and about to fly away and start building their own nests!

There was one more piece of mis-information that Pat Tom wanted to divulge to the neighbours as soon as possible. He went on his *cuaird* several nights but the opportunity never presented itself. Then one night an elderly farmer, sitting in the corner by the fire with his ash-plant stick leaning against the hob, began to condemn the young generation. 'They're as bold as brass,' he complained. 'Always wanting to do things their own way and they won't listen to us that know better. I can see it coming that they'll soon be picking their own husbands or wives. They are all talking now about these love-matches. Faith, love won't boil the kettle! They'll ruin the country, that's what they'll do. Sure the place is going to the dogs!'

Pat Tom saw the opening he had been waiting for. 'Be gor, I'm a bit inclined to agree with you, Jack. The way 'tis now, 'tis the father is the last to be told anything. It was only the other day that I heard, totally by accident, that our Kitty has been keeping company, a "strong line" they call it, with a young fellow from the far side of Ennistymon. There's even talk that it will be a hit, mind you. Several times the word came of proposals for a good match for her but she kicked the traces every time and wouldn't budge. Women can be fierce headstrong, you know. 'Tis a fright to God going up that far when she had plenty of chances near home.'

It was now out in the open. It would add to the stature of Kitty that she had found her own man.

After all the planning and scheming, everything went without a hitch. Young Paddy got married and Mary was delighted with her new daughter-in-law; she appeared to be enjoying life for the first time in many years. Early in the new year, the writings were drawn up for Kitty and Michael's marriage. That same night, Pat Tom and Mary gave the traditional party, the 'picking the gander', in Kitty's honour, with a gander killed and roasted for the occasion. It was an old tradition that while the local women plucked or picked the gander, the bride-to-be had to endure much teasing and leg-pulling about her wedding night. The wedding itself was a huge success with neighbours and relations of both families enjoying a magnificent feast, followed by dancing, singing and drinking until the break of day.

Kitty was extremely happy in her new home and raised a lovely family. While it was remarked by many that it turned out to be a marriage blessed by heaven, it could easily have been branded with an invisible stamp, 'Made in Lisdoonvarna'!

CHAPTER 7

Myths from the Past

THE TWIN AGES of technology and communications are upon us. The global village is a reality. Without moving from our livingrooms we can hear and see events as they happen in far-off places around the world. By simply pushing a series of numbers on our phones, we can talk to distant friends and relatives. The wonderful gadgets of technology are our servants though many of us have become slaves to these servants. And all this has happened in one short generation. But this explosion of technology, has, like any other explosion, left some casualties in its wake. Despite the joy and pleasure provided for us by radio and television, they have slowly but surely eroded one of the main characteristics of Irish rural life.

The art of conversation, within the home and among neighbours around the fire, was the central pillar upon which the survival of rural culture was based. For centuries, the traditions, stories, customs and beliefs of the people remained alive and vibrant. Now they are under threat. But one beneficial result of the arrival of a more enlightened age was the virtual disappearance of a great number of beliefs and superstitions. By today's standards, many of the old beliefs would be considered outlandish or even laughable but they were taken very seriously by past generations; as recently as the 1940s, those beliefs were still secretly feared by the small-farm community.

In general terms, the old beliefs could be divided into two main categories, positive and negative, or good and bad ones. Money was extremely scarce among struggling small farmers during the 1940s and nobody would consider sending for a doctor or a vet except as a last resort. It was then that most of the positive beliefs were encountered. There was always somebody in every neighbourhood who had a particular cure for the cattle's ailments, and was often considered to be better than any vet. Such people had a genuine knowledge of illnesses in cattle and had secret folk cures which were handed down from father to son. A few of the cures called for the dosing of a cow with several pints of stout, liberally laced with ginger, herbs or other secret potions. The inebriated cow usually showed marked signs of improvement once the hang-over had worn off.

Nor were people excluded from receiving excellent treatment. The untrained but instinctive skill of the local bone-setter, for instance, has often been an embarrassment to the medical world. In every parish, certain families had handed down folk cures for a variety of ailments ranging from ringworm, to stomach trouble, to migraine headaches or back pains. Many involved the use of home-made ointments or poultices, the ingredients of which were a closely-guarded family secret. Some of the cures, especially for stress-related problems or severe headaches, involved religious symbols only – a lighted blessed candle, holy water, the laying-on of hands and the recitation of certain prayers – and were, in all probability, the forerunner of the cures of the modern-day faithhealer.

But there was a dark side to traditional rural life. For centuries the people had been deeply religious, cherishing a simple black-and-white faith. Just as their way of life was an endless struggle to survive, the spiritual life was also seen as a struggle, a struggle of good versus evil, with all good things – good luck – coming from God and misfortunes – bad luck – coming from the forces of evil. Wishing a friend or neighbour good luck was a sign of faith and was embodied in normal conversation and in everyday greetings:'God bless all here' on entering a house, 'God bless the work', or 'That's a fine cow, God bless her'.

The fear of having bad luck led to a multitude of superstitions and beliefs which were perpetuated by the conversations around the fires. Flowing from their strong spiritual faith, the rural people loved the fireside stories of spirits, of haunted houses and fields, of ghosts, of the *banshee* and of the powers of certain priests to banish evil spirits and bring good luck to families. The guarded tones with which they spoke about those in the area who were alleged to have the power to bring bad luck on their neighbours, only served to increase the fear of such evil doing. They were so fearful of the dreaded practice of *piseogs* that they were nervous of speaking freely about them in case they should tempt fate. Any conversation on the subject was usually prefaced with a fervent, 'Wisha God preserve us from all such harm but ...'

The origin of *piseogs* is lost in the mists of time but it has been suggested that they were the last link with the ancient druids of pre-Christian Ireland. It was said that *piseogs* were used for one of two purposes. The first was to transfer, through some strange power, the good luck of a particular neighbour on to the person who was using *piseogs*. If a neighbour visited a house while butter was being made, for example, he or she was expected to turn the handle of the churn a few times as a gesture of good-will. Failure to comply with this custom, especially by a neighbour who was suspected of being involved in *piseogs*, was viewed with great suspicion. It was believed that through *piseogs* the butter could be stolen in some mysterious way, giving the *piseogs* user a two-fold supply of butter in his or her own churn.

The second use of *piseogs* was much more direct and malicious: to bring bad luck and even devastation to a neighbour and his family, to his livestock and his crops. The most extreme of such malicious practices, motivated by either jealousy or revenge, was the alleged ability to send a plague to the home and farm of an intended victim. As a boy I heard of one such frightening incident being recalled by neighbours as they gathered around the fire at night. Though the event was said to have happened around the turn of the century, it was still vividly remembered by a few old men from a neighbouring parish.

In an area of small farms, it was quite common for several farmhouses to share the same avenue or 'boreen'. In this particular case, four houses shared the same little road, one close to the main road and the other three scattered at intervals over a distance of about two hundred yards. One of the possible reasons put forward for later events was that there had been a major confrontation between the family in the third house and another family about a mile away over a disastrous love affair. Efforts to arrange a face-saving hasty marriage had failed. The family in the third house had refused to allow their son and heir to marry the unfortunate girl as she had no dowry and therefore was not considered good enough. The girl left home in disgrace, never to return.

Some time afterwards on a dull November evening, the farmer in the house nearest the main road noticed something moving towards him along the narrow boreen. As it came closer, he was transfixed with fear and revulsion. It was a long column of rats, about two hundred in number and travelling four or five abreast in a most orderly fashion. He grabbed a shovel to protect himself and whistled for his dog but the cavalcade went past his house and continued along the boreen. Bringing up the rear were two big rats, each holding one end of a long green rush in its mouth. Though this latter point was discussed for years afterwards, the only conclusion reached was that one of the rats was blind and was being cared for by the other.

The rats continued their journey, past the second house, and stopped at the third house. The house and sheds became infested with the plague of rats, though the neighbours on either side were left untouched. The rats gnawed through doors and ceiling boards, and invaded the kitchen and every bedroom until it reached the point where the family were afraid to sleep at night. In the sheds some of the cows choked themselves in their restraining chains in a frenzy of fear of their loathsome visitors while others aborted their unborn calves. The family's supply of vegetables for the long winter, the storage pits of potatoes and turnips in the kitchen garden, were also infested and devastated. The family made every effort to rid themselves of the rats but to no avail. No matter how many were killed, the numbers never seemed to decrease. One morning, five or six weeks later, the rats disappeared. Nobody saw them leave. They simply vanished and never came back. Where did the migration of rats come from – where did they go? Why did they infest only one house? Was the plague the result of *piseogs* or was it just a freak accident of nature?

Even as late as the 1940s it was hinted in conversations around the fire that in almost every neighbourhood, there was somebody, usually a woman, who was 'full of *piseogs*', and occasionally performed one of the rituals in some form or other. Outwardly, the alleged practitioners of *piseogs* appeared no different from anybody else, were always at Sunday mass and paid their dues. In an insular society, some people were always on the look-out for what were considered tell-tale signs. The finger of suspicion was often pointed, rightly or wrongly, at a person who never used a 'God bless' in his or her greeting. Certain people were often accused of possessing an evil eye which could bring illness to an animal by merely looking at it. It was significant that every farmer made a point of sprinkling holy water on his house, land and livestock on the eve of May Day and Halloween, two very important dates in the *piseogs* calendar.

This precaution was followed, at daybreak on May morning, by the tying of a branch of the Maybush to the rafters over the front door to bring good luck and to act as an antidote to any subversive *piseogs* activity of the previous night. The Maybush, the common furze bush, heralded the coming of summer by being the first to blossom, re-awakening the hibernating hedgerows in a blaze of yellow flowers. Though people denied the existence of *piseogs*, they felt it would be prudent to take precautions just in case they were wrong!

In a neighbouring parish, Pat the Yank lived with his wife and family on a very comfortable farm, He had returned to Ireland in the late 1920s after spending three years in New York. His two gold-capped teeth in the front of his mouth proclaimed to the world that he was a returned Yank. He had shrewdly saved the money he had made in America and expanded the farm that he inherited from his father and was, by this time, the proud owner of fifteen cows. By local standards, this elevated him to the status of a big farmer, a title which appealed to his not inconsiderable vanity. His one irritation was his next-door neighbour, Nell Rua, whose way of life did not conform to what Pat considered should be a woman's role. A large rough woman, she ran her household with an iron hand and could work in the fields with any man in the locality. Her small farm barely supported the six cows which were her only source of income. Possibly because of her flaming red hair, it was widely hinted that she had the power to practise *piseogs* though there was never the slightest shred of evidence to support such malicious rumours.

When Pat the Yank went on his *cuaird* at night, the other neighbours tried to keep the conversation away from the topic of good milking cows. Pat prided himself on the quality of his cows and, given the slightest opening, would bore his listeners on the subject. He kept a meticulous record on each of his fifteen cows in a dog-eared notebook which he always carried in his inside coat pocket, next to his creamery book. Given any opportunity, he would whip out his notebook and quote facts and figures on milk yields and butterfat contents to his unappreciative audience.

However, during one particular milking season, Pat the Yank became a very worried man. Now he frequently consulted his notebook in private but no longer in public. His longstanding good luck with his cows seemed to have taken a definite downward swing. His records showed him that most of his cows had a significant drop in their milk yield for no apparent reason and, of course, this was reflected in his creamery cheque. They appeared perfectly healthy, grazing contentedly in their field every day and every night. Pat was both worried and perplexed. To increase the yield, he fed them extra rations of crushed oats, cabbage and turnips. The cows relished the extra attention but their milk yield remained the same. He had his vet come to examine and test them but he found nothing wrong. Each cow was dosed with different mixtures and tonics but to no avail. An inspector from the Department of Agriculture arrived to test the soil for mineral deficiency but this was not the cause of the problem. It was a mysterious ailment that bordered on the supernatural. Despite Pat's unwillingness to talk about his problem, all the neighbours were aware of it because eagle-sharp eyes on the weighing platform at the creamery missed very little!

While Pat was on his *cuaird* one night, one of the group mentioned that the cow he had bought at a recent fair was one of the best milk producers he had ever owned. Another neighbour took up the conversation. 'Speaking of good milkers,' he said, 'Nell Rua must have the best six cows in the county. I helped her lift the milk tank from the pony cart on a few mornings and, upon my soul, I could hardly move it, it was so heavy. They must be powerful cows altogether.'

Pat the Yank listened and wondered how six scraggly cows could produce so much milk. As he walked home in the darkness, a sudden, terrible thought struck him. He had always guffawed at the rumours about Nell Rua and the *piseogs*. But what if they were true? He felt a cold shiver down his back. He recalled some of the stories he had heard since boyhood of persons using *piseogs* to transfer the good luck or the productive powers of another's animals to their own. What if Nell Rua had used *piseogs* to transfer the high milk yield of his cows to hers? The more he pondered on it, the more he became convinced that Nell Rua and her evil powers were the cause of all his troubles.

Before going to bed that night, he went to the field by the road where the cows were lying down in the high grass, some dazing and some contently chewing the cud. He gave them all a good splash of holy water. The following day he invited the local curate to bless the herd. He and his family began to bombard heaven with prayers and supplications to remove the curse that had ruined his herd.

A little more than a week later, Pat attended the wake of an old family friend. As was the custom, the neighbours showed their respect for the dead man and their support for his family by sitting up all night by the fire. At about three o'clock in the morning, Pat and another neighbour cycled the few miles home in the pale moonlight. As they neared home they passed by the cows' field. Pat was a little surprised to see all the cows standing up. Suddenly he felt an icy grip of fear as he saw two shadowy figures moving through the long grass in his direction. His companion also saw the figures and, whipping off his cap, he blessed himself. They stood rooted to the ground.

The figures came closer to the gap in the fence, one moving behind the other. Pat suddenly put all thoughts of ghosts and spirits out of his head as he recognised the leading figure. It was Nell Rua, closely followed by her son Con. Both were carrying two flowing buckets of fresh milk. Pat accosted her with a roar of anger as she climbed over the fence, expertly balancing the two buckets and a rather heated exchange followed! Pat swore to her that he would have her in jail before the week was out.

Nell Rua, envious of Pat's large herd, had decided to boost her small creamery cheque by partially milking Pat's cows in the middle of the night and had assumed that any fall-off in the milk yield would pass unnoticed. She enlisted the willing help of her son Con, on whom she doted, but whom many of the neighbours felt was 'a slippery bucko with all the makings of a right hoor'.

Pat was delighted that his cows were back to normal and that the mystery of the missing milk had been solved. He was so relieved that *piseogs* were not involved in his temporary misfortunes that he decided not to press charges against Nell Rua. Privately he felt that should the case appear in court, the simplicity of how he was duped and defrauded would make him the laughing stock of the area. A dignified retreat was better than a bad stand! And the neighbours sitting around the fire also gained from the experience because Pat the Yank never afterwards wanted to talk about milk yields. His dog-eared notebook never again appeared in public!

CHAPTER 8

In the Valley of Misfortune

ONE COULD NOT HELP but admire the neatly thatched house on the side of the hill. The bright whitewash on the house and on its surrounding stone fence, the freshly painted doors and windows, caught the eye of every passerby on the nearby road. The yard around the house was paved with a thick carpet of fine gravel as was the short boreen leading to the main road. Even the five-bar gate at the roadside was painted regularly. The neatness of the house and yard was reflected in the farm itself. The fields were well drained and free of rushes, or fellestroms, the fences were well maintained and an iron gate stood across the entrance to each field. It set an example for others to follow.

Seán and Maureen were a very happy couple. Though they were both originally from a neighbouring parish, they had lived on this farm since their marriage ten years previously and their three young children had been born in the renovated farmhouse. Following the death of the former owner, an old bachelor, his nephew in America had decided to sell the farm by public auction. The parents of Seán and Maureen had joined forces to purchase the run-down farm for the newly weds. Though several of the neighbours had an interest in buying the land, 'if it came handy, at the right price', there was no evidence of any resentment when the young couple moved into the old farmhouse. All the neighbours welcomed them, apart from one person who clearly disliked the arrival of outsiders and felt that he should have been sold the farm at a special price because of his friendship with the old owner.

Farming was a labour of love to Seán and Maureen. Within a short time they had transformed the dilapidated old house into a warm, snug home, newly thatched and whitewashed. Seán was an extremely hard worker and very progressive. The improvements to the farm amazed his neighbours. Fields were drained and fenced, gates were erected and, through good management, the quality of the land had improved to the point where it now carried ten highly productive cows where seven had been the norm. He also proved to be a great neighbour, always willing to give a helping hand when needed.

After ten years of good relations with his new friends and neighbours, only one unpleasant incident had occurred. The one surly neighbour who had not welcomed their arrival shared with them the use of a narrow lane. The little lane was the only means of access Seán had to his potato and vegetable gardens. Probably motivated by long-simmering resentment and some degree of envy, the neighbour blocked Seán's right-of-way with strands of barbed wire and bushes and refused to allow him to use the lane. A protracted dispute followed and, unfortunately, developed into a court case. Seán's rights were vindicated and the neighbour was bound to the peace for twelve months.

The year after the court proceedings, a strange series of incidents began to happen. During late spring, Seán was working in the potato garden with the horse and plough, raising fresh earth around the long drills of sturdy potato stalks. Close to the headland, the plough carved its way through a cluster of eggs which were hidden under a light covering of black earth. The stench of rotten eggs immediately filled the air. Seán attached no importance to the incident, assuming that one of his own hens had chosen the quiet furrows of the garden to lay her eggs, rather than the haybarn with the rest of the hens. A week later, his healthy five-year-old horse suddenly developed a cholic and died before help could be found. Later, at harvest time, under the usual green foliage of stalks, Seán was horrified to discover that his entire potato crop had failed, leaving him nothing but drill after drill of rotting, under-developed potatoes.

As the summer passed, Seán found several clutches of eggs, in the fields, in the cow sheds and in the garden. He instinctively felt that an errant hen could not be responsible for the incidents and that something strange was happening. Each time he found more eggs, he picked them up in anger and threw them into the clumps of briars on the fences. One morning, in the cows' pasture, he found six or seven animal bones placed in a circle with the white skull of some small animal in the centre. With his pitchfork he threw the strange collection of bones into the hedgerow nearby. Shortly afterwards, a mysterious illness struck his cows and one by one they died. The vet failed to diagnose the cause of death. Disaster followed disaster. Seán felt that somebody must have put a curse on him. It is natural for a farmer to suffer a minor setback from time to time, some small misfortune or other, but never of this magnitude. Ten years of hard work was being erased and he was powerless to stop it!

Without good neighbours, the family would not have survived. They helped Seán save the hay and fill the haybarn. Each of them gave him several bagfuls of potatoes, turnips and other vegetables to replace his own failed crops. With a little financial help from their own people, Seán and Maureen began to replace the lost cows, one at a time. Some young calves were bought in the hope of rebuilding their herd. But a few weeks later, Seán found one of the new cows dead in the corner of the field though she had appeared perfectly healthy the previous evening. To add to his misfortune, the three cows that remained of his original herd aborted their unborn calves, depriving him of his main source of income during the following spring. His bad luck seemed destined to continue.

His friends were convinced that somebody or other was using *piseogs* to ruin Seán. While the neighbours rallied around to help him as much as possible, they were fearful that the outbreak of *piseogs* would spread to their own farms. The items found by Seán on his land were traditionally the symbols of the dreaded practice of *piseogs*. It was a time of fear and suspicion. Several men avoided going on their *cuaird* at night rather than risk accidentally meeting the perpetrator of the *piseogs* as he or she went about the evil business. They privately urged Seán to go and discuss the whole affair with a local elderly priest who was regarded as a walking saint. But Seán dismissed their suggestions and could not bring himself to believe in *piseogs* which he regarded as long-gone ancient superstitions.

Towards the end of the harvest Seán drove his depleted herd of cows and young calves into the lush after-grass of one of his meadows. For several weeks, no animal had died and he prayed that the scourge would not return. Despite his attitude to *piseogs*, he walked every yard of the meadow searching for any hidden eggs or bones but found nothing. Three or four mornings later he went to the dew-drenched meadow to drive the cows to the sheds for the early morning milking. A short distance inside the gate, he came to an abrupt stop. He felt a cold shiver of fear as he saw, in the long grass, a rough circle of animal bones with a pyramid of about a dozen eggs in the centre. They had not been there the previous evening. His first impulse was to kick them out of his way but he resisted the temptation. Perhaps it was a figment of his imagination but he felt an aura of something evil around him. He remembered the saintly old priest.

After telling Maureen about his grisly find, Seán cycled to the priest's house. The old man listened attentively to the long litany of misfortunes that had befallen him and the numerous findings of eggs and bones. Seán almost expected the old priest to give him a tongue-lashing for even mentioning the word *piseogs* but he remained silent. He quietly told Seán to go home and wait for his arrival in his pony and trap.

A short time later the priest arrived at Seán's house and together they walked down the hill to the meadow. 'I just wanted you to see them for yourself, Father, before I threw them over the ditch,' Seán said as he stepped forward with a shovel to remove the eggs and bones.

'DON'T TOUCH THEM,' the priest almost screamed at him. 'Go back to the haybarn and bring me a good lump of hay or straw and be quick about it.'

He opened his breviary and began to pray as Seán hurried up the hill to get what had been ordered. He returned within a few minutes carrying a large bundle of hay on his back. 'Leave it there on the ground and I'll take care of the rest,' said the priest. 'And you stand over by the gate and keep the cattle away from here.'

Very carefully the priest covered the bones and eggs with the hay until it was piled up into a small pyramid. From a pocket of his long, faded, black soutane he produced a box of matches. Shielding a lighted match in his cupped hands, he walked around the pyramid of hay, touching the base at several points until there was a circle of fire. Satisfied that the hay was fully ignited, he stepped back a few paces. Wisps of white smoke rose from the bright flames around the base.

The flames licked upwards until soon the whole mound of hay was ablaze. The fire burned quietly for a few moments. Suddenly a belch of black smoke burst from the centre of the mound, showering a cascade of sparks over the surrounding area. Blue and purple jets of flame shot towards the sky. Seán felt the blood drain from his face as he gazed in awe at the fury of the fire. How could an armful of hay make such a raging bonfire? A thick column of black smoke, flecked with bright-burning sparks, rose to perhaps a hundred feet over the meadow. It formed a menacing mushroom-shaped dark cloud in which billows of smoke turned, twisted and writhed as though they were alive. A revolting stench filled the air, forcing Seán to retreat further and further though the priest never moved, still deep in prayer.

For at least a half-hour, the fire continued to burn, sizzling and crackling. Then, as suddenly as it had started, the flames died, leaving behind a smouldering pile of ashes. The thick pall of smoke vanished in the autumn breeze and the sun shone once more on that corner of the meadow. Stunned, Seán approached the man in black standing beside the fire. He looked at the priest in amazement. He was haggard and drawn, his sweat-streaked face smudged from the smoke and his soutane covered in soot and ash. He seemed utterly drained and exhausted.

'In the name of God, Father,' Seán asked him. 'What happened at all? I never saw a fire like that in my life. It was unnatural!'

The priest looked at him. 'What happened?' he repeated. 'It doesn't really matter what happened. All that matters is that your troubles are now behind you and you'll have no further problems. You have my word on that.'

They walked slowly up the hill to the house, each lost in his own deep thoughts.

As the priest had told him, Seán's long spell of bad luck ended. His cattle thrived and by the following year his fields and gardens were producing better crops than ever before. His period of hardship was past but the stress and the agony would never be forgotten.

He knew that something very strange had happened in the meadow. In many ways, he felt that he had been a witness to an invisible battle. A battle in which he was not certain of the identity of the combatants or the reasons for the conflict. Was his run of misfortunes merely an extreme case of bad luck? Or was it possible that some of the neighbours were correct in their suggestion that his troubles were the result of *piseogs*? Seán did not know. The happenings in the meadow had such a profound effect on him that he refused to talk about them to anybody, at least not for several years afterwards. But he was no longer as adamant in his denial of the existence of *piseogs* as he had been. He was no longer sure.

CHAPTER 9

The Joys of a Train Boy

AS CHILDREN OF THE '40S, our world had well-defined borders. It was about ten miles wide, from Mount Callan to the Atlantic coast, and about twenty miles long, from the banks of the Shannon to Ennistymon on the edge of the Burren. This may sound isolated and insular. It was both. Geographically, our area was cut off from the mainstream of Irish life. Surrounded on three sides by water, it was situated on the road to nowhere. Even our train service, the oft maligned narrow-gauge west Clare railway, reached the end of the line at a humble siding in Ennis station, unable to proceed any further. On the rare occasions when we happened to be at Ennis station, we would watch with envy as giant engines thundered arrogantly past on the nearby wide tracks, hissing jets of steam and belching smoke in our faces. Those trains of the Great Southern Railway seemed to look down disdainfully as they swept past our small engine and run-down carriages.

They would arrive from Sligo or Galway on their way to towns and cities that were but names on a map or a railway timetable – Limerick Junction, Cork, Waterford, Portarlington or Kingsbridge Station in Dublin. When they stopped at the station, we could see, through the open doors, the plush seats, the heated carriages, the dining car and the narrow corridor through which one could walk the length of the train while it travelled.

On the scale of passenger comfort, our local train would not have rated very highly. There was no corridor. The seats were hard with very thin padding, covered in faded, often torn, material. Ill-fitting doors ensured a constant supply of draughts. The system of heating was to put it mildly, antiquated and unusual. Long, sealed tin cylinders of water were heated in a boilerhouse in Ennis before the designated departure time. One cylinder was then placed in the space under each seat to warm the carriage and its passengers, but of course by the time the little train had huffed and puffed its way about ten miles down the line, all semblance of heat had vanished under the onslaught of draughts from doors and windows.

But despite its many shortcomings and discomforts, the west Clare railway had a certain charisma and held a unique position in the hearts of the people who lived within sight and sound of its tracks. Just as the people themselves felt ignored and isolated from the mainstream of Irish life, they felt that the west Clare line was being similiarly treated in the corridors of power. This created a common bond, a great rapport between the train and the general public of the countryside. It was as though the train was a living being and was struggling to survive like everybody else. Every success, however minor, achieved by the train was their achievement also.

Because of the desperate fuel problem and the resultant lack of pace, every hill to be climbed was a challenge to the train. The crew and passengers seemed to will it up every incline and exulted with it on reaching the top. It was looked on as a friend, as ours, and was stoutly defended against disparaging remarks from outsiders. Its many idiosyncrasies such as being tardy at times or having an untimely breakdown, were graciously forgiven with remarks such as: 'Ah sure, we all have our little failings and weaknesses.' Its supporters were quick to point out that, unlike its big brothers on the mainline tracks, it maintained a full service throughout the war.

This was an amazing achievement. The great shortage of imported coal during the war years forced the railway company to curtail its national services. The allotment of coal made available to the west Clare line was tiny and usually of very poor quality, mostly coal dust or slack. But a substitute was near at hand. The turf bogs of south-west Clare provided the answer as well as giving a badly needed boost to many a family income. In addition to cutting and saving their own supply of turf, people grasped the opportunity to save an extra couple of wagonloads for the railway and earn a few pounds. Of course, in terms of reaching the necessary high temperatures within the engine, turf was a poor substitute for coal. Sometimes this was further aggravated by a few greedy suppliers who increased the weight of the turf and their margin of profit by including wet turf in the centre of their wagonloads, well camouflaged by a layer of dry black sods. The unfortunate fireman on the engine then had to work exceptionally hard to keep up a head of steam.

The crews who worked the trains were held in high esteem. They were members of a close-knit group of railway people, living within the larger close-knit community. Sons followed fathers into jobs with the line. Linesmen, gatekeepers, porters, firemen, drivers and station masters were often second and third generation employees. The stations were connected by an internal telephone system which helped to create further bonds of friendship between fellow workers, and many of them bent company rules by relaying messages for the general public when the matter was urgent.

The west Clare railway was the lifeline of its catchment area especially during the war years. All goods for the different shops arrived at the local station and were collected from the store beside the station by horse carts or even by donkey and cart. On entering one of those storehouses, one was greeted by a combination of pleasant aromas and vast assortments of items. Plywood chests of tea, bags of sugar, grocery items packed in boxes and cartons, were neatly stacked in one corner. Bales of shovels and spades, rolls of fencing wire, boxes of nails, some hardware and items of furniture had their own section. Pride of place along one wall was reserved for the weekly delivery of stout to the local public houses. The sturdy timber casks, reinforced with iron hoops and painted with red lead, were stacked on their sides in a low pyramid, with the bung corks uppermost to avoid leakage. Occasionally the corks leaked, adding to the pungent aroma within the store. On a few occasions, the corks 'accidentally' came loose, when an unsupervised thirsty caller failed to resist the temptation of a free sample of the black liquid!

But for several generations of schoolboys, the west Clare trains held a special kind of magic. As a small child attending the antiquated two-room national school at Clonadrum beside the railway tracks, I watched the passing trains each day. Each train provided us with a momentary break from the tedium of schoolwork, because its rattle and roar silenced the master or missus for a minute. We watched the flashing windows of the carriages, envying the passengers as they rode along in what we considered the lap of luxury. The passing train conveyed an air of adventure and mystery. It was our Sante Fe, our very own Orient Express. I hoped that when I had completed my national school education, my parents could afford to send me to secondary school, the Christian Brothers in Ennistymon, because then I would get to travel on the train every day. It seemed a very good reason for attending secondary school!

For several generations of aspiring students, the west Clare train made secondary education a reality. Apart from Kilrush in the south by the banks of the Shannon, there was no second-level school along the coast and the inland residential colleges were beyond the financial reach of most parents. Those were the days before free education, of course. The morning train carried at least fifty students to the Ennistymon station and brought them back to their own stations each evening. To be one of the select group became my greatest ambition. It would be worth any price, any sacrifice.

Before giving us holidays at the end of fifth class, the master announced that despite his many doubts and misgivings, the whole class was being promoted to sixth for the coming year. We had reached the pinnacle! We had climbed the mountain! We actually looked forward to returning to school on the first week in September to savour the prestige and the power of being in the senior class. From our exalted position we would take no nonsense from those inferior beings in third and fourth class and would be graciously tolerant, well, up to a point, of the cry babies in the missus' room who would both admire and fear us. Maybe at the end of my sixth-class year, Mother and Dad would send me on the train to the Brothers.

It was a great summer and it passed quickly. On the Saturday morning before school re-opened, we were having breakfast at the big kitchen table at home. Having reached the ripe old age of eleven and being about to enter sixth class, I felt that I should begin to talk and act in a more mature, responsible way. 'Two more days,' I said in what I believed was a grown-up, casual voice, 'and I'll be back to school for my final year.'

After exchanging glances with Mother, Dad replied, 'We were just about to tell you a little bit of news. We talked it over with the master and have decided to start you off at the Christian Brothers in Ennistymon the middle of next week. The superior up there thinks that you may have to do an extra year at some stage along the line because you are so young, but he feels that this is a good time for you to start off in secondary school.'

I could not believe my good fortune. I was ecstatic! Who cared about 'being too young' or 'doing an extra year'? The great news was that I would now be travelling on the train every day. Everything else about going to the Brothers was of secondary importance, mere details! I could hardly wait to meet my classmates at mass on the Sunday morning. While I would miss the fun in the schoolyard, I knew that all the boys would be very impressed with my unexpected promotion.

The next few days seemed like an eternity as I waited for Wednesday morning to arrive, my first day going to school by train. I could not but feel a certain degree of superiority as I watched my former fellow-students trudge reluctantly back to school on the Monday morning to renew acquaintance with the missus and master. My old, canvas schoolbag was sent into retirement and Dad got the local saddler to make me a large leather bag with a long shoulder strap. To ensure my sartorial elegance, Mother decided that I should wear my Sunday best going to school each day – jacket, shirt, short trousers, pullover and long socks with the turned-down tops.

I seized the opportunity to give a broad hint that this was the ideal time for my first pair of low shoes. Mother appeared to waver a little, but Dad obstinately refused to budge from his belief that low shoes were not good for my feet and that I should wait until I was a few years older. End of discussion. The comfortable but far-from-elegant laced leather boots were destined to be my companions for at least another year.

On the Wednesday morning I arrived at the station more than a half-hour before the train was due. It was at least ten minutes before Mick the Station opened the waitingroom door. His sleep-heavy eyes betrayed the fact that he had only just got out of bed as he bade me a grumpy 'good morning'. Mick was a jolly, happy man with a great sense of humour but I quickly discovered that the morning was not the best time of his day. As train time approached, six or seven other students arrived, including two beginners like myself. From behind the rolling hills to the south came the plaintive whistle of the train as it left the neighbouring station, Craggaknock. Mick stuck his head around the partly-open office door. 'For Christ's sake, will somebody open the bloody gates before she runs through them!' he roared at us. Startled, we hastened to comply with his instructions.

We could hear the 'chug-chug' of the engine as it laboured up the slight incline a half mile away. On reaching the top of the little hill, it proclaimed its victory over adversity with a short 'toot' of the whistle. Partly hidden in billows of black smoke, it emerged from the final cutting in the small hill outside the station and came to a halt at the platform with screeching brakes and hissing jets of steam. Two or three heads packed each open window, shouting a variety of greetings to old school companions and quickly appraising the new crop of train boys. Doors were opened for us and we climbed on board. I was lucky to get a seat by a window. Charlie the Guard walked by, checking that all the doors were locked, before waving his green flag at Christy the Driver. The engine began to move and, with a series of jerks as the couplings took the strain, we left the little platform behind us.

I was seated in a double compartment, divided by a low timber partition, with a bulbous glass gaslight fixture attached to the ceiling. The pull-up windows had obviously been fitted with new leather pull-straps during the summer holidays though I heard somebody remark that: 'It was a pure waste of time because they won't last a week.'

There was a great babble of conversation as the events of the summer holidays were recalled and a few funny incidents of school life during the previous year were retold. It was rumoured that one or two of the Brothers had been transferred and all seemed to hope and pray that one Brother in particular whom they referred to as 'Steevo', had moved to greener pastures. Steevo seemed to be a holy terror. Somebody remarked that it was impossible to stay in his good books for more than a week and that one needed to be an Einstein to attain the standards that he, not alone expected, but forcibly demanded. It was obvious from the comments that he had a special set on train boys whom he appeared to consider uncouth, undisciplined, unruly and 'as thick as two planks'. I began to wonder if my great adventure was going to be the fun trip I had anticipated. The nearer the train carried me to the Brothers, the more pleasant and charming did my old teacher, the master, seem.

While the hubbub of conversation continued around me, I watched the changing countryside through the window. At each station large groups of students awaited our arrival. I was most impressed with the station in Miltown which seemed very big, with a glass canopy covering the platform. As we sped down the Black Hill, the beautiful scenery of Liscannor Bay spread out below us, with the Cliffs of Moher in the background. Conversation became subdued as we crossed the high iron bridge and came to a halt at the platform in Ennistymon. It was a quiet cavalcade that walked slowly out of the station and wound its way along Circular Road, with the senior students in the vanguard. From being one of the big lads in national school, I felt very small again, as if I was once more back in high infants. The seniors looked like adults to me, with long trousers, serious faces and bulging satchels of books.

Judging by all the books they have to carry, I thought to myself, they must be extremely intelligent and clever.

As we rounded the corner of the fair green, the high grey walls of the monastery towered over us like a fortress on top of a hill. 'Back again to Mount St Joseph,' somebody said in a voice of resignation. 'Abandon hope all ye who enter here,' quoted another dismally. A small dark figure appeared at the top of the steep lane leading to the classrooms. 'Oh Jaysus, Steevo is waiting for us,' somebody groaned. The pace immediately quickened. It was my first glimpse of a Christian Brother, in his long black habit and dark grey sash.

'Huh, train boys,' were his first words. 'The same old rubbish again this year, I see.' Most of the students laughed at his favourite annual joke. He seemed a nice mild-mannered man, though a little stern. Perhaps all those stories on the train were untrue or exaggerated out of all proportion? Only time would tell.

By the end of the first day I had come to the conclusion that life in a secondary school was much easier than national school and promised to be a pleasant experience. About thirty of us took our seats in the large first-year room. I tried to get one of the seats at the back of the class but some of the bigger boys pushed me out of the way and quickly established that coveted area as their own territory, forcing me, and my equally small companions, to occupy the unpopular front rows, I was finding secondary school strange in several ways. I was amazed to discover that each teacher taught his own particular subject only, thereby giving us constant variety. On that first day, we found them all very pleasant. They chatted to us, asking us our names and all about our previous schools. Even Steevo, despite a very dry sense of humour, did his best to put us at ease. However, it became rather clear from conversations in the classroom and in the playground that, within the student body itself, a three-tiered caste system existed, the townies, the country boys and the train boys. And that was the descending order!

In the evening, before we left for home, the superior gave the congregated train boys a stern lecture about our future conduct on the train. It struck me as rather amusing because Dad had given me an almost identical lecture the previous night. Judging by the model behaviour of all the students on the morning train, I felt that the lecture was quite unnecessary. Back at the station, which boasted two platforms, we waited impatiently for the overdue train to arrive.

'I hope it's the No. 8 engine we have this evening,' some train expert remarked. 'If 'tis the No. 3 or the No. 5, we'll be all evening climbing the Black Hill.'

I did not know that engines could differ from one another. All I wanted was to get on the train, enjoy the ride and get home as quickly as possible to show off my three new books, the Irish book *Séadhna*, a mathematics textbook and *Longman's Latin Grammar, Book One*.

The train arrived. A big red figure '3' on the front panel brought a mixture of groans and muted curses from the waiting students. We again found seats in a double compartment. The level of noise was much higher than on the morning trip, as much laughter, shouting and banter filled the carriages. The prophets were partially right because the antiquated engine crawled up the Black Hill.

The rhythmic, laboured chugging of the engine was soon augmented by the chorus of student voices singing an encouraging verse of 'Will-she-do-it, Won't-she-do-it, Sure-she-might.'

In our compartment all was quiet, well, reasonably quiet. As the train struggled up the big hill, a few pellets of paper were lobbed over the low partition from the very noisy compartment next door. A further hail of missiles followed, bread crusts, butts of apples and sundry pieces of rolled-up paper. Soon a loaded schoolbag came sailing over, landing on someone's head, and was followed shortly by its angry owner, bundled unceremoniously over the partition by his boisterous companions. Retrieving his property, he clambered back again, bent on revenge. A loud pushing-and-shoving melée began next door but subsided quickly as the train reached the top of the incline and cruised into the next station. For the rest of the journey there were no further outbreaks of horseplay.

My first day at the Brothers was educational in more ways than I had expected. The ride to school on the west Clare train had been wonderful but I had also discovered that there was a sting in the tail. I gathered from the talks given us by the teachers that a most unwelcome amount of study was expected. Entertaining a few misgivings about my newly acquired status, I sat by the fire that night trying to memorise my first Latin word, *mensa, mensa, mensam*.

Over time, the initial glamour of travelling to school on the 'west Clare' wore off but was replaced by a special bond which each of us felt with the old train. We came to know all its weaknesses and foibles. We came to pray that we would have the worst and weakest No. 3 engine on certain mornings, especially if we were scheduled to have Steevo for Latin or Maths for the first class of the morning; the good old No. 3 guaranteed our being at least half-an-hour late. We came to hate the lively No. 8 on those particular mornings!

Just as there was a certain bond between the west Clare and each student, there was also a special bond between the students who travelled together on the train, a kind of brotherhood of train boys. Our low-rated social status at school helped to establish an us-against-the-rest attitude. We were a little proud of being labelled 'wild and unruly' as it gave us a certain degree of prestige and was a definite deterrent against any acts of agression by outsiders. The real truth was that our toughness was a well-nurtured image which we all helped to perpetuate, telling stories to our gullible fellow students of wild rampages on the train.

About halfway through my secondary school years, we lost a trusted and much-loved friend. The familiar old west Clare steam engines were forced into retirement in the name of progress, and were replaced by a highly efficient but totally characterless diesel train. The spell was broken. The old magic was gone. It was bad enough that the new train was clean, quiet, warm and fast but worst of all from our point of view, it was disgustingly punctual!

CHAPTER 10

The Trials of a Cattle Jobber

THE OLD FAIR DAY is gone. Selling cattle in today's world of marts, sales rings and auctioneers has become a very organised business, governed by a complex network of rules and regulations. Fair day in the towns and villages may now appear to many as presenting a very romantic picture of rural Ireland in the past, but to the small farmers of the period it was vital to their survival. The monthly cheque from the creamery during the milking season paid the normal household expenses for the year. But with very few exceptions, farmers needed to sell their few surplus cattle to meet the extra annual demands and rates.

Selling cattle at a fair demanded its own skills. It called for shrewdness, experience and endless patience. It was like a game of poker, with the cattle as the stakes. In little groups of three or four, the cattle were walked into the town through the darkness of the night, arriving before dawn. The more experienced farmers tried to put their cattle on display near the centre of the main street, that being the area most frequented by the buyers. Good location was important because it was a buyers' market – a handful of buyers and a townful of restless, bellowing cows, yearlings and calves.

After a hearty breakfast in the local hostelry, the cattle buyers, usually from the lush grasslands of the midlands, strolled along the packed, heaving street. They were easily recognisable in what seemed to be their uniform, a wide-brimmed felt hat, an expensive warm overcoat with a fur collar and a well-polished ash-plant with a shining steel ferrule on the end. The buying or selling of cattle had developed into a fine art.

When a buyer saw cattle that appealed to him, he walked around them a few times, examining them closely and silently for any bad points or weaknesses. With an obvious display of feigned disinterest, he then casually enquired, 'What are you asking for the cattle?' The farmer, with equal disinterest, quoted a price. Shaking his head in disbelief, the buyer told the farmer that his asking price was outrageous, and then walked away. Within a half-hour, he returned, making an unacceptably low bid on the cattle. He might well leave and return several times, raising his offer a little each time while the farmer responded by lowering his price a pound or two. Eventually when a compromise price seemed possible, the real haggling took place with other farmers in the area joining in to help clinch the deal. The noisy talking would lead a stranger into believing that a fight was taking place. The willing helpers were enjoying the thrill of making a successful sale for their fellow-farmer at a reasonable price, with the traditional few shillings, the lucky penny, to the buyer.

At every fair, the top quality cattle were bought by the cattle buyers in the first spate of selling, but the second rate or inferior cattle posed a problem. The unfortunate owner of poor quality cattle needed an intermediary or middle-man to help him make a sale. This fringe element of every fair was the cattle jobber who made a few pounds by introducing a buyer to a farmer and helping to finalise the deal. The jobber usually began in the business as a drover, herding the purchased cattle for the cattle buyer to the local railway station and loading them into the cattle wagons. The jobber was an expert at haggling and making a sale, using a variety of skills and techniques to break down stubborn barriers to reach a compromise. Sometimes they graduated to buying a few inferior cattle at rock-bottom prices at the close of a fair, in the hope of selling them for a few pounds' profit at the next fair. Though they may have been considered fringe players, they fulfilled an important role in the cattle trade and their gift of the gab and quick wit made them great characters in their own right, welcome at any fair and at every fireside.

About fifteen miles from our house was a large, market town, well-known for its big fairs. Some distance up a lane off the main street of the town lived twin brothers on their own in a small house. They were cattle jobbers. At the rear of the house was a large yard, filled with an assortment of junk, broken-down farm machinery, cart wheels, pieces of timber, rusted sheets of galvanised iron, empty tar barrels and so on, all of which had been collected by the brothers in their travels, in the hope of re-selling at a profit.

The elderly bachelor brothers had been christened by a proud mother, possibly in a flush of Apostolic enthusiasm, as Bartholemew and Matthew, but were known to everybody as Battie and Mattie. They were the best-known and most popular cattle jobbers in the county, attending every fair in their efforts to make a meagre living. Like addicted gamblers, they dreamed of that elusive coup, the big sale, that would lift them to the ranks of the major cattle dealers.

The twins were well-known for their persuasive powers in achieving a sale for a grateful farmer. Their witty comments were quoted around many a fireside and even the dour no-nonsense cattle dealers enjoyed their jokes, their stories and their great sense of humour. By injecting a few good laughs into a bargaining session, they usually got both parties into a good mood, making the completion of a sale much easier.

My father, who originally came from the same area of the county as the twins, had known them since he was a boy and held them in high esteem. They were regular visitors to our house especially on their way home from a local fair. Mother always prepared a meal for them and, despite their permanently dire financial straits, Battie never failed to bring a few pence worth of hard cane sweets for me. Needless to mention, I was always delighted to see them, not only for the little bag of bulls' eyes but because of the fact that, unlike many other adults, they always held a conversation with me, often telling me stories about my father when he was a small boy. Well-known for their love of a bottle of stout, every pocket of their jackets and overcoats seemed to hold at least one bottle of their favourite beverage, all of which they would generously share with their friends.

After finishing a dinner of perhaps bacon, cabbage and

potatoes, Battie and Mattie would sit around the fire with Dad and Mother for a chat. As usual, a few neighbours would arrive on their *cuaird* and a good night's entertainment was assured. Battie would regale his audience with stories of their escapades at fairs, of their wheelings and dealings or of some great scheme that could have made them a fortune except for some small miscalculation or touch of misfortune. Battie was clearly the boss and the spokesman for the partnership, doing most of the talking, with Mattie nodding his head in agreement and enjoying the stories and jokes as though he was hearing them for the first time.

They were a harmless good-natured pair who managed to survive in the harsh world of cattle dealing. Basically honest in their dealings, it was generally accepted that one should show a little extra care when buying an animal from them. While they never told deliberate lies about an animal, they often sinned by omission, forgetting to mention certain relevant facts such as age or general health condition, facts which, if known, devalue the animal!

My father often recalled meeting up with Battie and Mattie at a local fair one day. During the fair they had bought a rather ancient cow at a very low price in the hope of making a pound or two in a quick sale. The excitement and activity of the fair was proving a little too much for the very thin cow as she stood by the kerb with drooping head and closed eyes. While they chatted, a cattle dealer casually strolled towards them, twirling his walking stick. Battie interrupted my father, 'Hold your whist there a minute, Paddy, there's a candidate coming towards us.'

The cattle dealer, on the look-out for a good bargain at

the close of the fair, walked slowly around the dozing cow, silently assessing from all angles her few remaining qualities. After a long pause he said to Battie, 'What are you asking for the old cow?'

Never one to answer a question directly, Battie replied, 'Well, sir, I'd be giving her away for nothing if I didn't get twenty pounds for her, she's such an honest cow and a great milker.'

'Do you know what?' said the dealer, 'I'll do you a favour and take her off your hands. I'll give you a five-pound note for the sleeping beauty.'

Without a moment's hesitation Battie retorted, 'Will you go away, boy. Sure, I wouldn't even wake her up for that much.'

Occasionally their scheme of buying poor quality old cows, for a quick sale and a small profit, backfired on the twins, leaving them to take care of the elderly matrons with hopes of a sale dwindling as day followed day. However, Battie and Mattie made an inspired decision to turn this misfortune into a new enterprise. They decided to get rid of their surplus stock by embarking on a new career as family butchers and make a small fortune by selling the fresh meat directly to the housewife on her own doorstep.

For the short time the new business survived, they travelled the countryside in their pony and trap. The two brothers sat on one side of their ramshackle trap from which the door had long since fallen off, while the other seat and the floor were piled high with chunks of beef, covered with a far-from-white bedsheet, a token gesture to hygiene. To keep matters as uncomplicated as possible, and because of their lack of knowledge of the where-abouts of fillets, steaks and sirloin in the carcase, they agreed that all their fresh meat should be sold as boiling beef only.

The initial round of calls on their new customers proved very profitable as delighted housewives wel-comed the new door-to-door service. Battie used the same sales approach at each door, 'Missus, would you like a lovely piece of fresh "mate" for boiling?' However, it was soon discovered that Battie's fresh meat had many unde-sirable qualities. Curses were piled liberally on the heads of Battie and Mattie as strong jaws tried in vain to chew it. It was boiled and re-boiled but the beef from Battie's old cows resisted all such puny efforts and remained as tough as shoe-leather.

The second visit of the travelling butchers was a painful experience for the enterprising twins. Irate housewives expressed their opinions in no uncertain terms, forcing Battie to call on all his experience to weather the storm. To each angry housewife he explained, 'Yerrah, missus, 'twas how the "mate" was too fresh. Give it a right good boiling this time and you won't know it. You'll eat your fingers after it!' As a gesture of goodwill, he dropped his prices, but there were very few repeat orders!

During their brief careers as butchers, the twins discov-ered that younger beef was needed to boost their vanish-ing sales figures. But young cattle were expensive and beyond their reach. Occasionally an animal suffered an injury on a farm. Should the injury be of a serious nature such as a broken leg, the animal was put down by the local vet, a total loss to the unfortunate farmer. In another one of his inspired moments, Battie saw an opportunity that might help save his declining business: if he could get to the farmyard before the arrival of the vet, he could buy the injured animal for a few pounds and have a supply of young beef for his customers that should keep them happy and contented for a while. Though this happened on a very irregular basis, it helped to prolong their careers in the meat business for just a little longer.

While Battie and Mattie may have had short careers as travelling butchers, they pioneered a service which was quickly imitated and carried on by others. Many of the qualified and successful butchers from the various towns followed the trail blazed by the twins. They visited each house on a regular basis, usually on Fridays or Saturdays, selling the various cuts and joints of meat to housewives who appreciated the good service and the good meat. This service survived in rural Ireland until the 1960s when going to town was made easier as cars became more plentiful.

CHAPTER 11

Entertainment
Highlights of the Year

THE CHILDREN OF THE '40s rarely suffered from boredom. There was always some activity for them especially during the long summer holidays, either helping with the farm work or else playing at some game or other. A child's imagination has no boundaries when it comes to games. He can be a soldier in the battlefield, he can be the captain of a big ship in a storm or a great naval battle. He can be a teacher, ranting and raving at an unruly group of imaginary pupils or, with a cloth ball and a piece of stick, he can become one of the great hurling or football heroes.

The housewife was kept busy with her normal housework during the day and often until late at night. Her work was not confined to the four walls of the kitchen. Quite apart from helping her husband in the hayfield, turf bog or potato garden, the fowl were her responsibility; she also fed the calves and the fattening pig and helped to milk the cows. At night, children were cared for and put to bed. Afterwards any quiet moments were spent either sewing or mending. Social life was an unheard-of luxury, apart from a rare visit to relations or a sick friend or, perhaps, during the day, a neighbour might drop in for a chat and a leisurely cup of tea.

Husbands had a slightly better social life, though few would admit it. Their Sunday visit to church very often included an hour or more in the nearby public house, talking with their friends over a few glasses of stout. Fair days and funerals also provided an opportunity for several social drinks. By far the most popular form of social activity for the husbands was their nightly visit to some neighbour's house on their *cuaird*, especially during the long, dark winter nights. Four or five of them would gather around the open turf fire, discussing world affairs, cattle prices, the occasional titbits of local scandal and the events of the day. Stories were told and yarns were spun about times past or about absent friends. Intricate family relationships and complicated marriage connections were traced, many of them going back over several generations. The night usually ended with a cup of tea and some homemade bread and jam. Shortly after finishing their tea, the lady of the house washed and dried the delph and replaced it carefully in the glasscase or on the old traditional dresser. This was acknowledged as a signal to the visitors that it was time to go home.

However, very few outlets of entertainment existed for single adults, those in their late teens or early twenties. A general scarcity of money was an accepted fact of life in rural Ireland but it was felt even more acutely by this particular age group. Almost all of them worked on the family farm and depended for pocket money on the goodwill of their parents who had very little to spare even in the best of times. Most nights were spent as bored but silent listeners to their elders around the fire. Perhaps once a week, they would gather in some house to play penny games of cards, either forty-five or spoilt comb, or walk to the village to meet their friends outside the lamp-lit window of the grocery shop. Dancing at the local parochial hall was their main past-time, if they had the money, especially in winter. Those who had girlfriends could rarely afford to take them to the dance but arranged to meet them inside the hall.

Their main source of dancing pleasure was the house dance. Those dances were organised for a variety of reasons, to welcome a family member home from abroad, for example, or to bid farewell to a departing emigrant – the American wake. There was always a Wren Dance, and sometimes a dance was organised by some local entrepreneur who would very quietly collect sixpence or a shilling at the door from the willing enthusiasts. More often than not the dance was organised by young family members just for a good night's fun and enjoyment. Usually they were invitation only dances but gatecrashers were graciously allowed to join in the fun. Tea, sweetcake and plenty of griddle cake with butter and jam was provided during the dance while the flagged kitchen floor reverberated to the rhythmic tapping until daybreak.

One very welcome visitor to our area, at the beginning of each summer, was Sam the Showman and his wife. They set up their amusements in a small field near the crossroads, staying for about a month before moving on a few miles to a site beside the village. Their gaily decorated horse-drawn caravan heralded the coming of summer. Some of the local men were delighted to give Sam a helping hand in erecting his two main, or rather his two only, attractions – a group of four swinging boats and a one-gun shooting gallery. 'Sam is back' the news would spread like wildfire and the crowds begin to gather shortly after milking time.

First came the children accompanied by at least one of their parents. At threepence a ride, the swinging boats were in constant demand under the watchful eye of Sam's wife. Sam's non-stop patter of jokes encouraged the fathers to test their skill with the well-worn pellet gun. The target was a postcard-size metal plate with a tiny hole in the centre, behind which a small bell was suspended. Should one succeed in ringing the bell, the prize was four free shots. 'Four shots for a tanner [sixpence],' Sam's voice boomed at intervals. On a small shelf beside the target was a jam-jar of thick whitewash and after each volley, Sam gave the target a quick swipe of a small whitewash brush to restore its clean image for the next marksman.

As darkness fell, it was time to take the children home. Sam placed four or five tilley lamps at different vantage points, two of which were suspended on ropes from the top tripods of the swinging boats. An old gramophone with a large trumpet-like horn blared scratchy background music from time to time. With the children and parents now safely out of the way, the little arcade became the focal point for most of the unmarried men and women within a radius of several miles. The boys, dressed in their Sunday clothes and with hair plastered firmly in place with brillantine, used the occasion to impress the girls. Getting into one of the boats, they pulled on the ropes with all their might, to drive their timber craft higher than the nearby competition to roars of encouragement from the crowds below. They took their girlfriends, or prospective girlfriends, for a swing. Squeals of delight and feigned fear rent the air amid shouts of 'Pull harder' and 'Higher, higher!' from the onlookers. At the end of the three-minute ride, the shrill voice of Sam's wife rang out, 'Hold your irons there, mister. She's landing.'

At the shooting gallery, Sam was kept busy running a competition, awarding the grand prize of a half-crown to the person with the highest score. To add a touch of class to the competition, he used ringed target cards and collected a fee of a shilling before carefully doling out five small lead pellets to each entrant. To claim the grand prize, the card showing the highest score had to include a bull's eye. However, the sights of the gun were rarely set properly and seemed to change slightly from night to night, keeping scores rather low especially on nights when the attendance was small! Night after night Sam's small arcade provided entertainment for those who had money to spend and for mere onlookers.

Unfortunately, I was never allowed to go to the amusements at night but I still managed to enjoy the thrill of the swinging boats, because the arcade was on my route home from school. For us schoolchildren on our way home, Sam had a specially reduced charge of a penny per ride. Experience taught us that even better value could be found if one had a bigger and heavier fifth or sixth class boy as a partner. Then with bare feet wedged securely against the pushing-block on the floor of the boat, we pulled on the ropes with all our might to swing in a high arc, though standing up in the boat to gain extra momentum was strictly forbidden by Sam. When the ride was over, I ran the rest of the way home to make up for lost time and thus avoid any awkward questions about being later than usual.

Shortly after the end of the war when some of the restrictions were lifted, a new and much more sophisticated form of entertainment arrived for a two-week stay at a little field in the local village. Hollywood had come to the west coast courtesy of Mister Mack's Touring Picture Company. Compared to Sam's humble arcade, this was a lavish extravaganza that took the whole area by storm, ensuring packed houses each night. The entourage boasted two ancient lorries and a caravan. The caravan doubled as a ticket office and a home for a coughing and wheezing generator that provided a stuttering supply of electricity.

For my part, initial approaches for permission to visit the travelling cinema fell on deaf ears. However, our good friend and next-door neighbour, Michael, interceded on my behalf and I was allowed to go with him. About seven o'clock the two of us set off to walk the mile-and-a-half to the village, with me trotting beside him to keep pace with his long adult strides. On reaching the top of the final hill a half-mile from the village, we could already hear the blare of tinny music in the distance. A large crowd had gathered, including a horde of children who chased each other around the guy ropes that supported the canvas roof of the cinema. One could sense an air of festivity and excitement. Michael pushed through the milling crowd at the ticket office window and purchased our tickets, his for a shilling and sixpence and mine for sixpence. We entered through the canvas flap at the rear corner of the cinema.

I looked around me in admiration. The sides were of

gaudily painted timber, surmounted by a twin-peaked canvas roof which was supported by two large poles, poles which were loudly cursed during the film for obstructing some people's view. A small stage occupied most of the front. This was to be a major production, first a stage show and then the pictures! Rows of long benches were placed on the grass and the children sat in the front while the adults' seats rose higher and higher all the way to the back. Within a matter of minutes the whole cinema, including the narrow aisles at each side, was packed. I could see Michael sitting at the end of a bench at the back. He waved to me and I felt very secure.

Over the noise of the chattering crowd could be heard the 'putt-putt-putt' of the spluttering generator. A few impatient shouts of 'C'mon, start her up', or 'We'll be here all night', rose up from the back of the cinema. At last, the filmsy stage-curtain was pulled aside and Mister Mack himself, dressed in a sequined black suit and a dicky bow, stepped on stage. In a thundering voice he welcomed us all and sang a comic song that got the crowd in a good mood. Two funny sketches were next on stage. Sandwiched in between the sketches a comedian with a fuzzy beard and an outrageous baggy suit made his appearance. I had a suspicion that it was Mister Mack again, but I was not too sure. He did pretend falls on stage, squirted water at the audience through a flower in his lapel and told a lot of jokes, many of which I did not understand though they brought loud guffaws and roars of approval from the back of the cinema.

The stage show finished with a couple of songs and some stepdancing from a small girl who must have been a wonderful dancer because her dress was almost covered with medals.

There was a short interval during which tickets were sold for a raffle. While this was going on, Mister Mack and another man hung what looked like a very big white bedsheet at the front of the stage. When the raffle was over, the lights went out and at last the film began. The first was a silent comedy with Charlie Chaplin, and there was non-stop laughter at his antics. The images flickered across the white screen, pale grey shapes slightly out of focus. Halfway through the film, the projector broke down, and we were plunged into darkness. Howls of protest rose from the audience. We all joined in the foot stamping and whistling though we were completely confident that Mister Mack would fix matters in no time. The next film was a short cowboy serial, *Burn-'em-up Barnes*, an episode of which was shown each night.

The main film of the night was the big favourite, a cowboy picture with Hopalong Cassidy. We all became totally engrossed in the great adventure. The fistfights in the saloon were cheered to the rafters while in the gunfights we worried for Hopalong's safety. We imagined ourselves standing shoulder to shoulder with our hero, shooting the bad guys with the black hats. In the heat of one gunfight, our ambushed hero got a warning shout from some excited spectator at the back of the cinema, 'Watch out behind you, Hopalong, there's another hoor with a gun on top of the roof.' He seemed to hear the warning and saw the danger in the nick of time!

At a very exciting point in the film, the generator coughed, spluttered and stopped, plunging the whole place into darkness again. Roars of frustration rose from the packed benches. A stream of curses was directed at the faulty generator, at Mister Mack, and back again at the generator. One of Mister Mack's assistants placed a lighted candle on a ledge by the front corner and shouted over the din that the picture would be back in a minute. Having watched the amazing marksmanship of Hopalong on the screen, the lighted candle offered an irresistable temptation to some of the tough guys at the back. One of them dug up a piece of earth with the heel of his shoe and took a pot-shot at the candle. He missed! Within seconds, several other sods, or scraws followed. The candle seemed to lead a charmed life!

A shower of scraws whizzed like missiles over our heads as several others at the back took up the challenge. The candle disappeared under the massive bombardment. But the pelting continued unabated; it seemed that more than half the audience got into the spirit of things. Yells of anger and pain rose from all sides as some of the flying scraws hit an unsuspecting target. Curiosity got the better of me and I looked over my shoulder only to get smacked on the side of my face with a hard scraw. My nose began to bleed profusely, adding to my woes of being temporarily blinded. It hurt much more than I was prepared to admit. I had a handkerchief of dubious whiteness with which I wiped away as much as possible of the gory cocktail of mud and blood, though the sting of the blow remained for some time.

The generator finally roared back to life and everyone settled down again. Using the age-old cure to stop a nosebleed, I held my head tilted back as far as possible.

This did not present too much of a problem because the makeshift screen was suspended immediately in front of my seat. My enjoyment of the remainder of Hopalong's exploits, however, was severely hampered by the sore nose and the painful right eye. There was a huge cheer at the end as Hopalong rode into the sunset. Mister Mack thanked us for coming and announced an even more exciting programme for the following night.

Michael was waiting for me near the exit. 'Great God almighty!' he exclaimed. 'What the hell happened to your face?'

I explained about being hit with the scraw. 'Your father will think that I didn't mind you and that you got into a fight with somebody,' he continued.

A surge of apprehension gripped me as I pondered on the consequences. Michael soaked the soggy handkerchief in a barrel of water that stood by the outside wall of the cinema and cleaned my aching face as best he could in the dim light.

'I'm afraid you'll have a beauty of a black eye in the morning,' he informed me. 'And your nose doesn't look too great either.'

What would Dad say? I felt his first suspicion would be that I had got into some argument with another boy and had come off second best. If he felt that I had misbehaved and had become involved in a fistfight, I would be murdered. I begged Michael to come home with me and explain to Dad what had happened. I was full of anxiety but Michael told Dad about my being accidentally hit with a scraw. Dad accepted the explanation without question, which is more than I can say for my classmates or the master the following morning. I tried to explain that my black eye was the result of an accident but I felt that very few believed my story. One of them had the temerity to tell me admiringly that I was much more of a hard man than he had imagined.

I had hoped that I could go with Michael to the pictures another night but I felt that the black eye had ruined my prospects. Dad seemed to find my black eye a little amusing, often referring to me as 'our little Joe Louis'. Discretion told me that I should abandon my film plans, at least for the present. When Mister Mack returned the following year, I would be better prepared and perhaps I might go to the pictures several nights. In the meantime, I had learned a host of new ideas for playing cowboys, thanks to Hopalong Cassidy and Burn-'em-up-Barnes.

CHAPTER 12

The Long and the Short of It

TO US, AS BOYS in the '40s, the boy's short trousers were a noble garment! They were the centrepiece of our ensemble. Shoes, stockings with turned-down tops, cotton vests, cardigans, pullovers and shirts were mere accessories and one or more could be discarded, depending on the weather. But the pair of trousers were a permanent fixture.

Traditionally boys had rarely worn underpants beneath their short trousers. Winter insulation was catered for by mothers sewing a heavy cotton lining to the inside of the trousers to protect the nether regions of their offspring against the dangers of frostbite. By the time I went to school, underpants had become quite fashionable. While fashion is all very well in its own place, in our schoolyard the wearing of underpants was considered effeminate by many of the hard men in the senior classes. Any accidental sighting of the offending cotton underpants led to a chorus of derisive shouts of 'Paddy is a girl. He's wearing knickers!' The unfortunate wearer of the underpants often suffered these humiliating insults and cat-calls for a week or more and was thereafter branded as a softee or a sissy who had little hope of ever graduating to hard man status. It was therefore imperative that mothers, despite their good intentions, were encouraged only to purchase underpants with a tight-fitting elastic waist and, above all, with the shortest possible leg. Any accidental flash of white cotton, even a half-inch below the trouser leg, was an invitation to disaster in the schoolyard.

In the turbulent '40s, the boy's short trousers were a basic garment. The waistband was loose-fitting with two buttons on either side of the front and two buttons on the back. The trousers were held in place by suspenders or braces which were securely buttoned to the waistband. Any button that popped off during the heat and rigours of a schoolyard football match was immediately picked up and brought safely home. Buttons were a very precious commodity in those years. Spools of thread were no longer to be found in the shops and the available skeins of hussive (housewife's) thread were of such poor quality that buttons were constantly falling off. Should any of us be so unfortunate as to lose both buttons from either side of the front or more especially from the back, a short nail or piece of wire kept our dignity intact until we reached home. The boy's trousers did not have loops for a belt. Only adult show-offs or shapers wore a belt, often with a large fancy silver buckle to impress the girls at the dances.

But with the modernisation of the '50s came the first hint of the belt for the boy's trousers. Its advent was almost unheralded because the simple addition of belt-loops gave one the option of either belt or braces or both. Tailors, in the interests of fashion and styling, unwittingly gave a major boost to the belt by sewing the suspender buttons on the inside of the waistband; this made the buttoning of the suspender-tabs much more awkward.

From that point onwards braces were doomed!

But the arrival of the belt was merely a tentative border-crossing in the War of the Trousers when compared with the up-coming invasion which was to engulf the manhood of Ireland. The traditional four or five buttons in the trouser-fly, after generations of loyal service, were being replaced by a cold, sharp-toothed, metallic monster, the zip, better known as the 'zipper'. Howls of anguish and pain re-echoed around the countryside from the mouths of the unwary. Swear words and curses rent the air from behind haystacks and furze-covered ditches as men, normally of quiet demeanour, struggled with the vagaries of this new contraption. Zippers continually got stuck in the half-mast position while others developed the embarrassing habit of flashing wide open at the slightest movement. This created a great strain on the wearer especially if he was in mixed company. Because of this ever-present threat to their dignity, men developed a nervous twitch as they constantly checked either visually or with lightning-fast unobtrusive touches to confirm that their zippers were behaving themselves in the proper manner. The wayward zipper undermined man's confidence in his own strength and invincibility and weakened his defences. But despite many teething problems, the trouser manufacturers inserted zippers in all their products and fly-buttons fell beneath the wheels of progress.

The boy's short trousers were a most liberated garment. By today's standards, the legs were quite long, coming to the top of the knee-cap or maybe an inch above it. The trousers were loose-fitting, giving maximum freedom of movement for running or playing. However, the poor quality of the tweed quickly revealed the Achilles' heel of the short trousers – the seat. The constant movement of backsides on hard school benches or the thrill of sliding down a hay-float in summer time rendered the trouser seats threadbare in a very short time. The material just grew thinner and thinner, as in the Dance of the Seven Veils. Before the point of total revelation was reached, mothers rescued the situation by stitching on a patch of good material, salvaged from a discarded trousers or jacket. The fact that the new patch rarely matched the herringbone pattern, or even the colour of the trousers, was of little consequence. Our trousers were serviceable once more! Our dignity was intact!

At school, we found that the mid-morning break and the half-hour lunchtime were far too short for what we considered was the primary purpose of going to school – playtime! Our quickly organised games of chasing each other or kicking a ball were precious to us, and necessary visits to the antiquated toilets at the back of the school were unwelcome interruptions at which no time should be wasted. In such moments of crisis, the loose leg of the trouser, proved invaluable, allowing one to bypass the time-consuming buttons and return to the field of play in the shortest possible time.

But there were other times of crisis when the same buttons were worth their weight in gold. There were occasions when shortcuts were taken with the homework. You took a calculated risk that the master might not have the time to check it or that he might only ask a few questions at random, skipping past you as you tried to look as inconspicuous as possible. Occasionally the gamble paid off. But such brinkmanship put a tremendous strain on the nervous system! More often than not, he started firing questions at one end of the class, working his way towards the other end. Even a quick abject Act of Contrition failed to divert the approaching doom.

The last slender hope of self-preservation was to take evasive action – raising the right hand to ask permission to go to the toilet. Judging the precise moment to request permission was an essential art that only came with experience. Raising one's hand too early meant that, even with delaying tactics, one came back from the toilet in time to face the unwelcome question. If left too late, the master first asked the hated question and then granted the now useless permission. Assuming that the timing was correct but that the upraised hand was ignored, one immediately moved to Plan B. A slight crouch was adopted, the face assumed a pained expression while the shuffling of the feet indicated a certain amount of discomfort. Re-application for permission was made immediately, with upraised hand.

Once permission was granted, the longest possible route to the toilets was chosen, walking all the way around the school building with measured, dragging footsteps. On reaching the toilets, the loose leg of the short trousers, which was so convenient during playtime, was now ignored. Instead, one slowly unfastened each button, ekeing every possible extra second from the operation. Through the open windows at the back of the school, it was possible to monitor the progress of the questioning by the master. When it appeared that the danger had passed for the moment, you slowly retraced your steps back to the classroom, making sure to be seen running past the master's window to indicate your great desire to continue with your education!

The threshold over which a boy steps from boyhood to manhood is a major milestone in the seven ages of man. The boy may have yearned for a few years to belong to the world of adults, yet he enters it while still looking over his shoulder. This giant step is recognised in the traditions of many cultures around the world. In the Jewish tradition, a boy celebrates his Bar Mitzvah shortly after reaching his thirteenth birthday. At the ceremony, he reads tracts from the scriptures and is publicly welcomed by his rabbi and his family to the world of adults: he is now recognised as a full member of the community. Ancient civilisations and cultures such as those found in Africa, India and the Americas also recognised the importance of this stage in a boy's life. Tribal customs call for initiation rites and special ceremonies to mark the occasion.

In the west of Ireland we had a much more simplistic approach to the occasion. The date of taking that first step into the world of grown-ups was not governed by one's date of birth nor was it marked by religious ceremonies or initiation rites. It was very simple and very practical: when one had outgrown the largest available boy's short trousers, one was brought to the local tailor to be measured for the badge of manhood and, to those of us still in short trousers, the ultimate symbol of authority and of the world of adults, the long trousers!

Our expectations were sublime. We secretly expected that our forthcoming long trousers would, like a magician's cloak, transform us from mere lanky boys into elegant grown-up men. We could then demand proper respect from our former peers and be in a position to look down on their infantile games of tig and football, with the disdain we had always associated with adults. We looked forward to being admitted into adult conversations where we would participate in sensible talk about current affairs, cattle prices or the latest local scandal. Perhaps we might even be allowed go on *cuaird* at night to a neighbour's house to discuss the local happenings and even give our thoughtful and learned opinions on such weighty matters as the merits or demerits of a neighbour's cow or horse. And to emphasise our new-found social upgrading and importance, we might even smoke a cigarette in front of our former peers instead of the few stolen drags of a shared cigarette butt behind some lowly shed. Naturally, mothers and fathers would have to be excluded from such an exhibition. Even our imaginations recognised certain limits.

However, the main preoccupation in graduating to long trousers centred around the delicate subject of girls. We felt that we knew all there was to know about girls. We had gone to school with them all our lives, since we had been in low infants. But they were so different from us! They chattered like a flock of chickens among themselves, giggling much of the time. Most of them had long hair, either in ringlets or decorated with ribbons and they became unreasonably bad-tempered if one of us goodnaturedly pulled off one of their ribbons. And from seeing them fall in the schoolyard, we knew that every single one of them wore knickers! They usually played what appeared to be very unexciting games among themselves, liberally punctated with high-pitched squeals of delight. Not enjoying the privilege of having sisters like most of the other boys, I noticed one big difference between boys and girls which, I had to admit, I liked very much. Should one of the girls fall in the schoolyard and begin to cry – they seemed to cry very easily – all the other girls gathered around to console her. On the other hand, if any of the boys had a painful fall, the shedding of unmanly tears was greeted with cat-calls and jeers.

But the worst thing about girls was that they were absolutely hopeless at football! Sometimes they joined us in a game but, despite the fact that it was well organised, it fell apart very quickly because they either did not know, or else could not follow, the simple rules of our game. It could be exasperating! Admittedly the girls were very friendly and were good company but, in our young eyes, they were – well – just girls! However, despite our early doubts, many foundations were laid in the schoolyard for friendships that have endured the passage of time.

Graduation to long trousers again raised the subject of girls. From our more streetwise schoolmates, we had heard oblique references to girlfriends. There seemed to be an endless litany of jokes and innuendo on the subject and we laughed and guffawed like everybody else. Unfortunately most of the jokes and comments were mysteries to us and evoked more curiosity than merriment. But to express ignorance on the matter or to ask questions was to invite the jibes and scorn of our knowledgeable peers. However, we were all aware of the fact that there was a very definite link between the wearing of long trousers and girls, or rather, girlfriends.

And this much talked-about experience of falling in love? To us it appeared to be some mild form of insanity or, at best, some kind of custom or ritual that was very popular among grown-ups, though it looked like a very boring past-time. We assured each other that we would never make fools of ourselves like certain people we knew and would have nothing to do with girls or any of that silly nonsense called love.

In a relatively short time after my fourteenth birthday my legs grew a few inches longer. The legs of the short trousers were let down to the limit but they were still far above the acceptable benchmark of the top of the knee-cap. My exasperated mother declared that she would have to get me a new suit with long trousers, especially for Sunday wear. Here was one of my dreams come true! I could already visualise myself strutting around in my long trousers, silently proclaiming to the world that I was now a man.

Mother and I cycled to the local town, five miles away, where a friend of hers had a draper's shop. The long narrow shop had its shelves packed from floor to ceiling with long flat bales of suit material. Much to my relief, they both decided that there was no need for a waistcoat which was, by that time, considered a little old-fashioned. So the new suit was now reduced to a two-piece, long trousers and a jacket, otherwise known in our area as a 'frock', a nickname that probably had lingered on in the vernacular from the far-off days of the long frock-coat. Bolts of material were opened on the well-worn counter and examined for quality and texture. The predominant material was the standard dark navy serge, renowned for its hard-wearing qualities. While I had but a passing interest in the quality, I hoped that the look on my face would betray my dislike for dark navy serge. I was delighted when Mother chose a light shade of blue, airforce blue which was the 'in' colour at the time. Once the makings, the required number of yards, had been cut from the bolt, the lady of the shop assembled the trimmings, buttons, thread, a new-fangled zipper, satin lining, padding for the shoulders and some light stiff canvas which was used to retain the shape of the lapels and the front of the jacket. We were ready for my first trip to Pat the Tailor at his workshop a little further up the street.

The tailor's shop was like a rather dark cave filled with clothes. Suits of clothes, at various stages of manufacture, lined the walls and overflowed on to long benches and over the backs of chairs. The scorched smell of ironing filled the room. On a huge square table, Pat the Tailor was busily ironing a large navy trousers with a heavy flat-iron. Clouds of hissing steam rose from the dampened garment and Pat wielded the heavy iron as though it was as light as a goosewing duster. Looking over the tops of his small steel-rimmed glasses, perched on the tip of his nose, he welcomed us. 'Wisha, you're very welcome to town, Alice,' he said. 'And I see you've brought the young man himself with you.' Instant recognition of my upcoming transition to manhood! I liked him already.

When he finished ironing the trousers, he examined our brown paper parcel of makings and trimmings. 'Tis a fine piece of stuff,' he commented. ''Twill make a grand suit. We'd better start measuring you, young man.'

He opened a dog-eared red notebook, selected a blank

page and sharpened a stump of a pencil with one blade of an outsize scissors. 'Now, my good man,' he said, turning to me, 'stand up straight, straighten your shoulders and stick out your chest and I'll throw the tape on for the jacket.' He worked quickly, measuring me for the jacket and then for the trousers, recording all the time and keeping up a rapid flow of conversation with my mother.

We returned a week later for a fitting. The same bewildering collection of suits lined the walls. I could see no label or name-tag on any of them and I wondered how Pat could identify each suit. Like a magician taking a rabbit out of a hat, he pulled my suit from the middle of a huge pile. I looked at the object he held in his hand. I was dumbfounded. I had seen better than this on a scarecrow in the middle of a field of oats. It was a disaster, festooned with a network of loose threads and odd-shaped pieces of canvas while the two sleeves were held in place with a couple of safety pins. Very gingerly I put on what he assured me was the jacket. He fussed around me with an old tobacco box full of straight pins, tucking in here, letting out there and criss-crossing everything with a piece of chalk. Mother and himself expressed their satisfaction with the progress but I failed to share their complacency. If they thought for a moment that I was going to wear this patchwork quilt of a jacket and be the laughing-stock of the neighbourhood, then they had better think again about it. I immediately decided that the only option for me was to continue to wear the short trousers, regardless of how tight they became, and postpone this manhood business indefinitely.

But a week later, Mother returned from town with a

large brown-paper parcel tied with twine. I could scarcely believe my eyes when she opened the parcel and showed me the new suit. It was beautiful. Despite all my misgivings, it was a perfect fit. I could hardly wait for Sunday to arrive to show off to the world that I had joined the ranks of the grown-ups. In keeping with my new status, I felt that I should begin to distance myself slowly over the next few days from all boys' games and practise talking in a serious adult vein. And I should also begin to read the newspaper so that I could discuss national and world affairs, however uninteresting and boring they might be. After all, that's what grown-ups did.

On that fateful Sunday morning in spring, getting ready for mass took longer than usual. This was a special day, the world premier of my first long trousers. To complete my own image of elegance personified, I had splurged sixpence on a slender bottle of brilliantine with which I liberally doused my hair. Mother did not appreciate my display of good taste and proceeded to wipe most of it off with a towel. My chest expanded with pride as I admired myself, resplendant in my new airforce blue suit, in the mirror on the door of the wardrobe. I was a man, a real man!

I decided against cycling to church, just in case the oily bicycle chain would stain my new trousers. Actually I felt it would have a much better effect if I walked casually into the village and gave the general public more time to admire and acknowledge my new status. As I walked along the road, I practised some of the poses I had seen in newspaper advertisements, first with one hand in the trouser pocket, then the other. Going towards the church,

I exchanged greetings with several neighbours and convinced myself that I had received many admiring glances. I avoided the front seats of the church where most of the boys, my former peers, were seated and chose instead an end seat midway in the long aisle, on the lefthand side, among the men. The lefthand side of the aisle was traditionally occupied by men only while the women used the righthand side. So far, so good! Everything was going according to plan.

But the clouds of doom and disaster were only minutes away. On leaving the church, I saw my former companions running around the street as they usually did. I impulsively started to follow them but suddenly realised that chasing youngsters up and down the street would be considered very undignified behaviour for an adult in long trousers. I walked sedately, and with as much dignity as I could muster, down the middle of the street to the shop where a group of the boys were gathered. My suit with the long trousers should be a sensation! I swaggered towards them but instead of the respect and admiration I expected, they all began grinning and guffawing at my sartorial elegance.

'There's the trousers but where is the man?' they shouted repeatedly like a well-trained chorus. 'What are you doing in your father's trousers?' jeered another. 'By gor, but you're a right little maneen in them trousers,' said somebody at the back of the group. Even though I was aware that such teasing occasionally took place, having participated myself once or twice, I believed that it could never happen to me. With a crimson face and a badly deflated ego, I beat a hasty retreat.

Determined to retrieve at least part of my dignity, I joined a group of men outside the church gates. The conversation stopped and they looked at me as though questioning my intrusion. 'Wisha, well wear to your new suit,' one of them said. I thanked him. Another said, with a condescending smile, 'God knows but you're a fine bit of a man in your long trousers.' They returned to their animated huddle and resumed their conversation, ignoring my existence and silently dismissing me from their circle. I was not one of them!

I walked home, deep in thought. I wished that I had never seen that blasted long trousers. What a fool I had been. And more than likely I had alienated all my old friends. It looked as though adulthood was a closed society which did not welcome new members. I was in a limbo between the two worlds. I could hardly wait to get home to change back to my old short trousers. Perhaps there was more to being an adult than just wearing long trousers. It was quite confusing. I still wanted, on the one hand, to play football and chase around the place with the boys while, on the other, I wanted to be taken seriously by the grown-ups.

When I reached home, Mother immediately noticed my dejected looks. I told her the whole story, of the teasing, the mocking and the jeers of the boys, and of being ignored by the adults. She understood my hurt feelings and encouraged me to have patience with both the boys and the men, as the transition from boyhood to manhood did not happen overnight and had very little to do with the wearing of long trousers. She reminded me that in between the stages of being a boy and being a man, there was the vital stage of being a youth, a stage which I had assumed I could skip over and ignore in my haste to become a man. I was delighted that I had talked out my problem with Mother. She was a good listener and was never dismissive. And she always had a simple solution for my problems. As she stood up from her chair beside the fire to begin preparing the Sunday dinner, she turned to me and said in her quiet, gentle voice, 'Never pretend to be what you're not. Always be yourself.' I can still hear her words as though it was yesterday.

CHAPTER 13

The Grand Dance

I WALKED SLOWLY to the railway station carrying my heavy leather schoolbag and an even heavier heart. It had been a great summer holiday. The new long trousers had been worn to mass each Sunday but it was back to 'old faithful', the short trousers, for the rest of the week. Most of the days had been spent driving the gentle horse, Grey Fann, arould the meadows with the hay-rake, the tosser and even the wide timber float which carried the haycocks from the meadow to the haybarn. Dad would still not allow me drive the mowing machine because not alone was it dangerous work, but he was afraid that I would push Grey Fann a little too hard. I noted from time to time that the legs of my short trousers were receding further and further from my knees, and I felt that this was my last summer of running barefoot along the dusty roads, that change was finally on its way.

In spite of my protestations, Mother bought me long, ready-made shop trousers for my return to school to begin my third year at the Brothers. I even took my case to the Supreme Court – Dad – but he sealed my fate with a few short words: 'You're wearing what your mother tells you and that's that!'

So here I was, trudging along the dusty road to the station, laden down with worries and half-hoping that the old west Clare engine would break down and fail to arrive. The prospects for the coming year looked exceptionally grim especially with that most difficult of examinations, the Intermediate Certificate, looming on the horizon! I said a silent prayer that one of my less-than-favourite Brothers had been transferred during the summer holidays, otherwise we would all be murdered for the rest of the year. And now, to add to my problems, here I was with these infernal long trousers holding my two legs in hot suffocating captivity. I tried to steel myself against the inevitable hoots of mockery and derision that I would surely have to suffer from my fellow students on the train.

The train arrived at the platform exactly on time. Two or three boys packed each open window. Shouts of greeting and welcome came from every side. Not one snide remark about the long trousers? This made me very suspicious! But I found the answer when I boarded the train. Most of my classmates were in the same predicament as myself – they too had switched to the long trousers. Relief flooded through me. Each of us tactfully avoided the subject of long trousers, so despite all my worries and forebodings it was a non-event!

The school term dragged on but the Christmas holidays finally arrived. It seemed that every school subject had become more and more difficult and there were a few occasions when we had fleeting moments of regret that we had not listened to our teachers with greater attention during the previous year. But somehow or other, we survived. Now we could relax and forget about studies for the holidays. For months I had been looking forward to visiting Aunt Liz, Paddy and my seven cousins for my annual Christmas holiday even though every broad hint to Dad brought the same depressing reply, 'Maybe it would be more in your line to mind your books.'

In the end he relented when I promised to study extremely hard on my return from Cooraclare. Time enough to worry about that later!

In due course I arrived at my aunt's house with my usual bag of extra clothing. In a separate parcel I carried my airforce blue new suit to wear to Sunday mass. Some of my cousins had not seen me before in long trousers but they tactfully said nothing. The fun was as good as ever. We danced a few sets each night and visited the neighbours' houses. Under the girls' patient coaching I had managed to become a most unspectacular set-dancer. While the quality left much to be desired, I could now stumble through the five figures of the set without disrupting the rhythm of the good dancers on the floor.

On Sunday morning I wore my new suit as I walked to mass in the village with five of my cousins. Unfortunately, Mai and Della were unable to come home for Christmas as they were on duty in their hospital in Waterford. After lunch, five of us, Anna, Lily, Eileen, Teresa and myself were in our usual huddle around the table, planning the night's entertainment. Anna and Lily had decided to go to a modern hall dance in Kilmihil and showed us the advertisement in the county paper that announced in bold print, 'Grand Dance in Kilmihil Hall. Music by Jack Madigan and his Band with amplification. Dancing 9 to 3. Admission 2/6.'

Eileen had planned to visit Tadg's, one of the neighbours, for a few sets, but now she wavered. The prospect of the sets grew dimmer when she decided to ask her dad to allow her go with her two sisters. Lily, drawing on her legal experience, argued that he would veto her request because Teresa and myself would be more or less abandoned. However, she suggested a solution to the problem. If all five of us were to go as a group, together with a few neighbours, permission should be forthcoming. I thought it was a wonderful idea because I had never even seen a modern dance. With my new suit I was ready for any occasion. I could visualise myself gliding across the floor with my arm around the waist of a beautiful partner, to the envy of the less-talented men and the admiring glances of the ladies. I would put Fred Astaire in the shade!

The more we talked, the more enthusiastic I became. However, getting permission could present a major problem. A variety of devious solutions were discussed and discarded. Eventually, settling for the direct approach, Anna and Lily were appointed ambassadors to undertake a diplomatic mission to the cowshed where Aunt Liz and Paddy were milking the cows. We held little hope of success. The waiting was unbearable but eventually they returned and their smiling faces told us the good news. Permission had been granted though there were several conditions as to our general conduct and the time we should get home. Anna and Lily were appointed our warders for the night with responsibility for our safety and well-being.

When our initial elation subsided a little, the girls decided to give me a crash course in the art of ballroom dancing. Eileen and Teresa were already excellent dancers, having learned the skills from their sisters but, alas, my dancing education had been sadly neglected. It was a blow to learn that no sets would be danced in the hall but I had a very basic acquaintance with the old-time waltz so at least that was a start. Eileen took me up on the floor for a little practice. One-two-three, one-two-three, one-two-three. No problem so far, though matters deteriorated rapidly.

The other girls supplied the music, lilting the popular songs of the day. I may have been a little familiar with the songs themselves from listening to the radio but the dance steps were an entirely different matter. Efforts to learn the foxtrot, the quickstep, the tango and the rhumba proved futile. Eileen tried valiantly but all these dances seemed very much alike to me. By tacit agreement the crash course was abandoned. Tactfully the girls assured me that over half the people in the hall would be beginners like myself. They advised me that when I took a girl on the floor, my best approach would be to observe the other dancers around me and follow their example. That seemed to be the ideal solution. Bursting with confidence, I had a feeling that my first modern dance was going to be a memorable one.

With the outside chores completed, the whole family gathered around the big kitchen table for supper. I was too excited about the Grand Dance to have any appetite for the food. I kept glancing at the clock on the wall. I had never seen that minute hand crawl so slowly around the big dial and I was only half listening to the good-humoured chatter around the table. Paddy's voice cut across my flights of fantasy. 'I suppose,' he said to me with a feigned look of innocence on his face, 'your father would be delighted if he knew you were going to a hall dance in Kilmihil tonight.'

A wave of panic engulfed me. How many times had Dad said that I would not be allowed to go to a hall dance until I had sat for my Leaving Certificate?

Oh, my God, I thought to myself, if he finds out that I've gone to a hall dance, there'll be holy war. I'll be murdered for sure.

I quickly calculated the distance from home to Kilmihil. It was over ten miles. But what if somebody from home was at the dance? What if they mentioned it to Dad? It would be the end of the world! I might never again be allowed visit my aunt's house. No! I would not risk it. I would stay at home!

The girls sensed my panic and tried to re-assemble my crumbling world by assuring me that Dad would never find out about the dance and, should the worst happen, they would tell him that they had forced me to go. I considered this carefully. It was not the ideal solution but it might be sufficient to stave off disaster. In some un-canny way Dad always seemed to sense or hear about my little indiscretions. But this was of major proportions. 'Oh well,' I thought, 'let the last day be the hardest!'

A little after eight o'clock, Eileen suggested that it was time to begin to get ready. Having no desire to keep my cousins waiting, I immediately went to my room, had a quick wash, changed my shirt and put on my new suit. I was ready in five minutes. I went back to the kitchen where Aunt Liz admired my suit and examined the qual-ity while Paddy teased me that 'all the girls at the dance will be mad about you'. There was frenzied activity as the girls got themselves ready, flitting across the kitchen, from room to room, from mirror to mirror. It was my first experience of girls getting dressed and ready for a dance. I kept glancing at the big clock and at the minute hand which now seemed to race around the dial, but I eventually resigned myself to the fact that the best part of the dance would be over by the time we would get there. Slowly the normal kitchen smells of the turf fire and of cooking surrendered to the exotic aroma of face powder, lipstick and perfume. Even Rusty the collie who had sneaked in the open kitchen door for a comfortable snooze by the warm fire lifted his head from the cushion of his paws and sniffed the air. Having decided that the pleasant fragrance did not represent a threat to his territory, he promptly went back to sleep.

The clock struck nine o'clock, the advertised starting time of the dance and still the preparations continued. I began to harbour grave doubts on the wisdom of proceeding further with our entertainment plans. I had just about decided that we should abandon our trip when the four girls emerged from the room. 'Now, that did not take long, did it?' one of them said. Paddy just smiled and winked at me. All four of them looked wonderful. Coats were quickly donned and the girls put on their headscarves to protect their well-styled hair-dos. It was a beautiful moonlit night, ideal for cycling. In this we were fortunate, because only Lily had a lamp on her bicycle and that only provided a glimmer of light because of its weak battery. As there was always the danger that we could meet an over-zealous Guard, we planned to park our bicycles in a farmyard outside the village and finish our journey on foot. Before reaching the main road, we were joined by four others – and still only one lamp!

Once we were on the main road the smooth tarred surface made cycling an easy task. My first instinct was to pedal furiously to make up for lost time but the others were in no hurry, enjoying the carefree conversation as we cycled two or three abreast with Lily and her flickering lamp in the vanguard. Should we be challenged and pursued by a Guard, we all felt that we had the speed and the stamina to out-cycle him.

However, such an emergency did not arise and we reached the outskirts of the village without mishap. We parked the bicycles at the back of a haybarn besides a farmer's house, hiding our lamp and our one bicycle pump in the hay at the side of the barn. A quick rub of a spare handkerchief removed most of the mud spatters from our shoes. As we walked into the village, we could already hear the sound of music floating over the rooftops. Little groups of people were still winding their way up the main street to the hall so I figured we were not too late after all. As we merged with the crowd in front of the ticket office, the girls said to me that I would be better off taking strangers up on the floor, at least for the first three or four dances, to give me confidence. I thought that what they suggested made good sense and I foresaw no difficulties. I had a feeling that I was going to have a very busy night on the floor.

At last we entered the hall. It was fantasy land! It was ablaze with light, electric light bulbs all along the walls and hanging from the ceiling. Through a forest of bobbing heads, I caught glimpses of the band at the far end. All six members of the band were resplendent in black tuxedoes and bow ties. I had never seen a modern dance band before and to me they looked like a group of filmstars that I had seen in some magazine. The ceiling was festooned with coloured streamers, and what looked like a huge revolving silvery football was suspended from the centre. One could sense the atmosphere of festivity and gaiety. The floor was packed with happy couples swaying and swirling to the fast tempo of a familiar tune. I watched in amazement from my position inside the door as an endless stream of couples sped past, ourstretched hands tightly clasped, foreheads glistening with perspiration and every person sporting a bright fixed smile. Modern dancing must be execeptionally enjoyable!

I watched, with some degree of misgiving, the ease with which they glided around the floor, even though I noticed that, unlike the traditional sets, no two couples seemed to employ the same footwork. But, against all that, they all appeared so expert and so relaxed! I began to doubt my ability to compete with their expertise. However, on closer inspection, I noticed that several of the men had a very tense look on their perspiring faces and danced with very jerky mechanical movements, lips moving as though they were counting. My confidence was restored. Eileen shouted in my ear that they were going to leave their coats in the cloakroom. 'When this dance is finished,' she instructed me, 'move up to the side of the hall and get yourself a partner for the next dance.'

The music stopped. The thunder of clapping rose from the crowded floor as the dancers applauded the band and each other. I thought this custom was most unusual because at the few house-dances I had seen it was always the onlookers who applauded the dancers at the end of a set. The couples separated on the floor, the girls going to the left side of the hall while the boys lined up, in places six or seven deep, on the righthand side. Some of the men whipped out a variety of coloured handkerchiefs to mop their brows; they would have used their sleeves for that purpose on any other occasion, I reflected. From where I stood, I could see the eyes of the men darting up and down the front row of girls on the opposite side, admiring, rejecting, considering, evaluating and eliminating. I made my way to the back of the crowd at the righthand side.

I looked up at the band. Jack, the leader of the band, leaned forward in his chair and tapped the microphone in front of him with his forefinger before announcing in a booming voice, 'Take your partners for a foxtrot!' Like an inexperienced racehorse, I was left standing at the starting gate. Within seconds, like the charge of the Light Brigade, the front ranks of the men dashed across the floor and grabbed their partners. Every girl was claimed, apart from a handful of unchosen ones who remained in their seats, staring up at the band, fiddling with their necklaces and trying to look unconcerned. I remained standing by the wall where I could observe the dancers and build up my courage for the next dance. I felt that I should wait for a slow dance before making my inaugural trip to the dance floor. I was learning the rules quickly and would not be left behind again. When the foxtrot ended, I jostled my way to the front of the crowd and, following their example, took good stock of the girls on the opposite side.

I immediately set my sights on a beautiful girl in a blue dress, with long wavy fair hair. The moment Jack announced the slow waltz, I sprinted across the slippery floor and stood beside her. Nerve and my voice failed me for a moment but, drawing a deep calming breath, I said to her in a croaking voice, 'Will you dance, miss?'

No response, no hint of recognition! Clearing my throat, I repeated in a louder voice, 'Would you like to dance, miss?'

Still no response! She kept staring at the stage, totally ignoring my presence and my request. This was frustrating. Before I had the opportunity to repeat my question, I was brushed to one side by a real sleazy-looking character in a light blue suit and a canary-coloured pullover, hair plastered down with brillantine. I took an instant dislike to him as he arrogantly leaned towards my chosen one and uttered just one word, 'Dance?'

Miraculously, she instantly recovered her hearing, got up and, without as much as a glance in my direction, walked to the centre of the floor with that dubious-looking character. I looked at her again. I decided that she was not really as good-looking as I had thought at first. Feeling a little dejected and rejected, I retreated to the other side of the hall to repair my bruised dignity.

It seemed a long time before the next slow dance was announced. This time I lowered my expectations and set my sights on a more 'comely maiden' who was sitting down in animated conversation with two other girls. A slow waltz was announced. I strutted across the floor displaying a confidence which I did not feel. I took a closer look at my second choice. There was no danger that she was on the way to Hollywood but, then, I had to start somewhere!

'Dance, miss?' I asked her in as deep a voice as I could muster.

'Haw?' she enquired.

'Would you like to dance, miss?' I repeated.

She gave me a long searching look. 'What in the name of God are you doing here at a dance, my little maneen? Does your mother know you're out?' she guffawed in a coarse voice. She followed this with a whispered comment to her two friends, who burst out laughing.

I was so embarrassed that I wished the ground would open up and swallow me. With crimson ears I retreated once more to my haven on the other side of the hall. This Grand Dance was fast becoming a grand disaster. Why hadn't I stayed at home? I saw my cousins on the floor having a great time. Several times they gave me elaborate hand signals, indicating that I should take a girl on to the floor for a dance. Little did they realise my problems!

For over an hour I watched the dancing, my confidence and my enjoyment at a low ebb. In fact I was beginning to feel rather miserable and quite sorry for myself. My ears throbbed from the rhythmic beat of the loud music. The heat magnified the contradictory smells of perspiration and cosmetics and even the fairyland mixture of lights and coloured streamers began to look tatty. Would the dance ever end? I looked at my watch. it was only a few minutes after midnight. Still about three hours to go! I felt that I should make a final effort to get on the dance floor. My misfortunes must surely have come to an end by this time. I quickly reviewed my strategy which was obviously all wrong, especially my expectations regarding dance partners. The 'top of the range' had got a sudden attack of deafness, while my 'middle of the range' choice had humiliated me. It appeared that my only chance of salvaging something of my first Grand Dance was to lower them even further, perhaps even to ground level.

I noticed one particular girl who had remained seated in the far corner all night, a permanent wallflower, though her friends seemed to be on the floor for every dance. From my vantage point across the floor she did not look underfed, her hefty shoulders shaking with laughter as she shared some joke with her friends. Even at that distance I could see that it would be a gross exaggeration to say that she was good looking! But I felt that we were kindred spirits, both of us failing so far to reach the dance floor. In a warm glow of magnanimous good nature, I decided that I would put an end to her miserable waiting and ask her for the next slow waltz. I waited impatiently for it to be announced so that I could perform my good deed and at the same time make my own long overdue breakthrough on to the dance floor.

The moment the slow waltz was anounced by Jack, I strode purposefully across the hall to the distant corner and stood in front of her.

'Would you like to dance, miss?' I asked her. She looked me up and down a couple of times.

'Heavenly Father,' she said in a gravelly voice. 'Is it how you want to get me arrested for cradle-snatching? 'Tis well past your bedtime, me bucko, so will you ever shag off for yourself and don't be bothering me. Come back to me when you start shaving.'

I darted into the crowd of dancing couples on the floor, and reached the relative safety of the distant wall. I felt very hurt, an utter failure.

My cousin Eileen saw what had happened to me and came across the hall to stand beside me. The look of dejection on my face must have been obvious. 'Don't worry about that girl refusing to dance with you,' she said. 'Anyway, that one causes trouble at every dance.'

She paused, waiting for a lull in the noise. 'I think we were wrong when we advised you earlier,' she continued. 'It being your first dance, you'd be better off dancing with all of us first before asking strangers. Come on to the dance floor with me now and we'll finish this dance.'

For the remainder of the night, each of my cousins danced with me and I began to enjoy the dance.

But the memory of those miserable first few hours lingered and I had many reservations about hall dances in general. I would not be in a hurry to attend another. Perhaps Dad was right, maybe I should wait until after my Leaving Cert! I hoped that he would not hear that I had broken his ruling.

On the stroke of three o'clock, the band played the national anthem. We all moved out of the hall, leaving behind the tinsel glitter of the grand dance for the cold, stark reality of the deserted village street. The moon had disappeared and the chilly darkness wrapped itself around us as we walked in a happy group to collect our bicycles. Now that the immediate need for spotless cleanliness had passed, we squelched through the thin layer of mud in the farmyard before reaching the back of the haybarn. Our bicycles were still there.

However, finding our hiding place for the lamp and the bicycle pump caused us some problems. We spent almost ten minutes searching the side of the hard-packed hay, groping with our hands until, at last, we found them. As we walked along by the side of the barn, I heard the rustling of hay and much whispering from high above our heads, inside the barn. I was startled for a moment but I suddenly realised that it probably was some people who had foolishly hidden their flashlamps on top of the hay instead of the side as we had done. Obviously they were not having much success in finding them because the rustling continued unabated. I felt a little sorry for them though it did seem very silly going to such extremes to hide their lamps.

I turned to Lily who was beside me. 'Don't you think,' I asked her, 'that we should climb up on the hay and help them find what they are looking for?'

In the dim light of her lamp, I saw the surprise on her face as she looked at me and asked, 'What are you talking about?'

'I think there are people up there in the hay,' I explained, 'and I believe that they can't find their bicycle lamps.'

'Well, God bless your innocent head,' she replied in a hoarse whisper. 'Come on home and let them find their own lamps, if that's what they're looking for. I don't think we'd get much thanks if we tried to help.'

I could see that she was shaking with silent laughter at my suggestion. I thought it was a little un-neighbourly not to even offer to help, nor could I see what she found so funny.

The journey home felt very short as we sang verses from every song, old and new, that we could remember. I found it almost impossible to go to sleep when I got to bed around four o'clock. I had never before been up so late. Overall, the night had been a disaster and I was totally disenchanted with modern dancing. The only further calamity that could happen was that my father would discover that I had been to the Grand Dance. He never did, though my feeling of guilt lasted a long, long time.

Other books from The O'Brien Press

LAND OF MY CRADLE DAYS
Recollections from a Country Childhood
Martin Morrissey
A touching and informative account of growing up in County Clare during the war years. Sensitive, detailed, moving story of a bygone era.
Paperback

OLD DAYS OLD WAYS
Olive Sharkey
Entertaining and informative illustrated folk history, recounting the old way of life in the home and on the land. Full of charm. *Paperback*

SMOKEY HOLLOW
Bob Quinn
A worm's eye view of how the fictitious Toner children managed to survive parents, neighbourhood and country in the dark ages before TV. 'A triumph ... Bob Quinn is a natural storyteller.' *Galway Advertiser*.
Paperback

THE HAUGHEY FILE
The Unprecedented Career and Last Years of The Boss
Stephen Collins
'Remarkably up-to-date ... fluent, well-written account of a rollercoaster period ... an outline of Irish history ... quite simply, a must.' *The Irish Times*.
Paperback

REVOLUTIONARY WOMAN
Kathleen Clarke
First-hand account of the most exciting period of Irish history. About her unusual life with her husband, Tom Clarke.
Paperback

KERRY WALKS
Written and illustrated by Kevin Corcoran
The book covers the major scenic areas of Kerry with 20 accessible walks around Kenmare, Dingle, The Iveragh Peninsula and North Kerry. Illustrated with the author's drawings and colour photographs.
Paperback

WEST CORK WALKS
Kevin Corcoran
Ten great walks in the wilds of West Cork - spread throughout the county from Macroom to Allihies. Learn about nature and wildlife with an expert.
Paperback.

FOLLOW YOUR DREAM
Daniel O'Donnell
Idolised by millions, Daniel O'Donnell became a legend in his twenties. This is his own story in his own words, taking the reader back to his origins, through his early days on the road and his life as an international superstar.
Paperback

DUBLIN BAY
From Killiney to Howth
Brian Lalor

With magnificent vistas in drawings and text. Takes us right around the bay from Killiney to Howth. *Hardback*

SLIGO
Land of Yeats' Desire
John Cowell

An evocative account of the history, literature, folklore and landscapes, with eight guided tours of the city and county. *Paperback*

A Valley of Kings
THE BOYNE
Henry Boylan

An inspired guide to the myths, magic and literature of this beautiful valley with its mysterious 5000-year-old monuments at Newgrange. Illustrated. *Paperback*

TRADITIONAL IRISH RECIPES
George L. Thomson

Handwritten in beautiful calligraphy, a collection of favourite recipes from the Irish tradition.
Paperback

DAIRYGOLD HOMES OF GOOD FOOD
Bibi Baskin

Recipes from the TV series – from Ireland's splendid country houses.
Paperback.

THE BLASKET ISLANDS
Next Parish America
Joan and Ray Stagles

The history, characters, social organisation, nature – all aspects of this most fascinating and historical of islands. Illustrated. *Paperback*

DUBLIN — One Thousand Years
Stephen Conlin

A short history of Dublin with unique full colour reconstruction drawings.
Paperback and hardback

CELTIC WAY OF LIFE

The social and political life of the Celts of early Ireland. A simple and popular history. Illustrated. *Paperback*

MARY ROBINSON
A President with a Purpose
Fergus Finlay

Fascinating account of the Robinson campaign. The making of a President as it really happened. *Paperback*

DUBLIN AS A WORK OF ART
Colm Lincoln

From the author of the popular *STEPS & STEEPLES: Cork at the turn of the Century*. Colm Lincoln provides a visual narrative of how the city came to be what it is today, with the aid of both archive material and new photographs specially commissioned by the National Library.
Black & white photographs by Alan O'Connor £19.95. Hardback